The Inscribed List

or

Why Librarians Are Crazy

The Inscribed List

or

Why Librarians Are Crazy

Hilarious Real Names of Real People from Library Catalogs

Eric v.d. Luft

➤➤ North Syracuse, New York ◄◄
◄◄ Gegensatz Press ➤➤
➤➤ 2008 ◄◄

"In loving memory of Richard Thibeault"

Cataloging in publication:

Luft, Eric v.d. (Eric von der), 1952-
   The inscribed list : or, why librarians are crazy : hilarious real names of real people from library catalogs / Eric v.d. Luft.
        p. : 18 cm.
        Includes bibliographical references.
        ISBN 978-1-933237-01-5 hardcover
        ISBN 978-1-933237-14-5 e-book
1. Authors—Humor. 2. Names, personal—Humor. 3. Books—Humor.
4. Titles of books—Humor. 5. Librarians—Humor. 6. Libraries—Humor
7. Literary curiosa—Humor. I. Title. II. Title: Why librarians are crazy.
        PN 6231 N24 L83i 2008   002.02/07—dc22   AACR2
Library of Congress Control Number 2007942710

First edition, first printing. Printed in the United States of America.

The guillemets, or two pairs of opposing chevrons, dark on the lower cusps and light on the upper, are a trademark of Gegensatz Press.

Distributed to the trade worldwide by:
Gegensatz Press
108 Deborah Lane
North Syracuse, NY 13212-1931
<www.gegensatzpress.com>

Cover by Saairah.
Interior design by Eric v.d. Luft.
Printed on acid-free paper. ∞

Preface

"Did you just say 'Balint Bakfart'???!!!???"

The first thing that ever happened to me the first time I ever worked in a library was that my supervisor, Richard, told me to sit down and listen to him read the entire contents of a bright orange catalog card box, which he had just pulled from its secret hiding place under the marking table. He said that he was going to "initiate" me into library life. I rolled my eyes skyward and grumbled to myself. There were about eight inches of three-by-five cards in that box, and I was not looking forward to being subjected to such tedium. I asked him if this ordeal was necessary. He assured me that it was — and that his boss, the department head, Joe, had personally approved it. I had never met Richard before, since my interview for the job had been with Joe. They both appeared to be decent enough fellows, but their plan to have me undergo a fraternity-style hazing just so that I could be privileged to mark books and file cards did not tend to endear them to me at all.

Sitting across the table from me, Richard solemnly informed me that his actual title in the library was not "Marking Table Man," but "Curator of the Inscribed List," that the box he was then opening was the repository of said list, one item per card, that all new student workers must have the Inscribed List read to them in full by the Curator, and that he was going to fulfil this obligation by reading it to me now. I resigned myself to a couple of dull hours of listening to the contents of all those cards.

I was just a Bowdoin College student who had been looking for a minimum-wage on-campus job between my junior and senior years. The assistant dean of students had asked me if I would like to work in the library. I said, "Sure, why not?" I had no idea what working a library would involve or whether or not I would like it.

There were six of us students working in the library that summer. We could — with the approval of the appropriate department head — choose which department we each wanted to be in. I had no idea what the various departments of a library were or did. So I picked cataloging because its department head, Joe, looked cool with his bright green slouch hat, scraggly little beard, sly winks, and warm smiles. I knew what cataloging was, but I didn't know what happened in cataloging departments or what catalogers did.

I was not in a good mood as I started that job. Within the past week I had had three impacted wisdom teeth and one non-impacted one chiseled and dynamited out under general anesthesia. I was still on super Tylenol hyped up with codeine, because my face was still swollen, purple, and throbbing. During a pre-operative consultation my dentist and my oral surgeon had had a loud twenty-minute argument in my presence about whether I had four or three wisdom teeth in my whole head and whether three, two, or one of them were impacted. This was not an incident to inspire a patient's confidence in the medico-dental hands into which he was being committed. The argument was still unresolved as I was rolled, supine, into the operating theatre, underdosed on pentothal. The last thing I remember was going into convulsions, trying to punch the doctor, and barfing on the table. When I awoke I learned that my oral surgeon had won the argument with my dentist. That information did not make me feel any better, and with my face greenish-yellowish-purple, fat, and aching, I was still not in the best frame of mind. To top it off, a few days later I discovered that that hopeless oral surgeon had left a suture in my mouth after he was supposed to have taken them all out. I decided to cut it out myself rather than deal with any of those bozos again.

Laughter was thus not on my agenda as I walked into the library that morning for my first day at work.

But within ten minutes I was splitting my sides, rolling with laughter, having quite forgotten my throbbing jaws and cynical outlook. The other workers didn't even look up — much. They had all seen and heard this sort of reaction to Richard's recitation many times before. For, you see, the Inscribed List is a selection in alphabetical order of real names, real book titles, and real subject headings from the main library catalog, the National Union Catalogs, OCLC, or any other recognized library authority. That might not sound very interesting to you — but wait until you see it.

Reading the box of cards took Richard an hour and a half, and by then my sides hurt so much from laughing that I could hardly walk, or even breathe. I instantly fell in love with librarianship, because I instantly learned that **librarians are crazy**. At least Joe and Richard were crazy — and they were the ones I would have to deal with that summer. I was going to have a great time there! Crazy people make the world fun!

That was 1973. The Inscribed List had been started just two years earlier when Joe discovered in the card catalog, quite by chance, the name "Increase Niles Tarbox." As soon as he stopped laughing, he decided to keep a separate file of funny names of authors, not only for his own amusement but also for that of his department and the library staff in general. He recruited other librarians with weird senses of humor to keep their eyes peeled to find other funny names in the card catalog for him. Soon he expanded the scope to include funny titles, funny author/title combinations, and funny subject headings.

Joe thus became the Founder and First Curator of the Inscribed List. But the demands of cataloging — the true backbone of any library — being what they are, Joe soon turned over the Curatorship of the Inscribed List to a kindred spirit, Richard.

Richard was the greatest of all Curators of the Inscribed List. Under his leadership the list rapidly grew and prospered. He was exceptionally vigorous in encouraging every clerk filing, every cataloger searching, every circulator circulating, every student worker shelving — indeed everyone with whom he had any contact in the library — to report to him any funny name, title, or subject heading encountered in the regular day's business.

When Richard changed careers he desig-
nated Dianne, who had been at the library
all along from the days of Increase Niles
Tarbox, as the next Curator of the Inscribed
List. She was also a very competent Curator, but, after Bowdoin promoted her from
Government Documents Assistant to Head
of Special Collections, she realized that she
did not have enough time for the Inscribed
List and so gave it back to Richard, even
though he was no longer a librarian.

Richard always believed that the Curator of
the Inscribed List should be a librarian,
simply because librarians have natural and
immediate access to those bibliographical
commodities by which the list grows: books,
MARC records, OCLC screens, union catalogs, subject authorities, name authorities,
OPACs, etc. When he appointed me the
new Curator — to supplement my remu-
nerated library duties — he stipulated that
I should transfer the list from file cards to
a database, print it out, and try to get it
published. I agreed wholeheartedly to these
conditions (especially since it was I who
had originally suggested them). But life in-
tervened. I did not get around to fulfilling
his mandate until now.

The Curators of the Inscribed List have
been:

1971-1972: Joseph J. Derbyshire
1972-1981: Richard Jude Thibeault
1981-1986: Dianne Gutscher
1986-1989: Richard Jude Thibeault
1989-present: Eric v.d. Luft

In each of the libraries where I have worked — Bowdoin College Library, Chester County (Pennsylvania) Public Library, and the libraries of Bryn Mawr College, the College of Physicians of Philadelphia, Syracuse University, the SUNY College of Environmental Science and Forestry, and Upstate Medical University — I have added to the Inscribed List whenever I have been able, and have asked my colleagues to help me. Among them I wish to thank, in addition to Joe, Richard, and Dianne, all the wonderful librarians[1] who have ever contributed to this list, especially Penny Schwind; Anne Campbell Slater; Rachel Levasseur; Jean Louise Gillis; Dean DeBolt; Diane Davis Luft; and Baroness Northover, *née* Lindsay Granshaw.

---

[1] To me, a "librarian" is anyone who has ever worked in a library, not necessarily a so-called "professional" with a Master of Library Science, Master of Information Studies, or some other essentially superfluous pseudo-academic degree. I say this as the holder of an M.L.S., who knows how worthless it is. In all the years I've had it, it has never helped me to do my job.

We librarians don't go deliberately looking for these little nuggets of delight. We don't have to. They just appear. Every librarian knows that. The accident of finding one of them while searching for something else, answering a reference question, or doing almost any of our daily tasks, is a keen source of the joy that characterizes librarianship in general. So don't worry, bosses. We are not wasting your time feeding our petty perversities. On the contrary, we are boosting morale. The Inscribed List builds knowledge of the collection, staff collegiality, and enterprise-wide solidarity!

Librarians don't file catalog cards anymore. We use electronic databases to track bibliographic information. But we still have plenty of opportunity to stumble upon funny names.

The Inscribed List contains mostly authors', illustrators', editors', compilers', translators', or composers' names, but also some titles, some author/title combinations, and a few subject headings. The only criteria for inclusion are that the entries be (1) real, authentic, and verifiable in library catalogs; and (2) funny. One of the main reasons that the list is so hilarious is that all the names are real. We do knowingly include pseudonyms unless we explicitly identify them as such — and even then we are reluctant to do so.

The Inscribed List is not only comic relief for librarians. The appearance of books by Russell Ash, Brian Lake, Michael Bell, and Larry Ashmead[2] indicates that a taste for childish humor exists within the general public as well as among bibliophiles. *The Inscribed List: or, Why Librarians Are Crazy* fits right in among these other compilations — with surprisingly little overlap.

Each entry is listed alphabetically, either by name, by title, by what used to be called the main entry, or by whatever element makes it funny. SUBJECT HEADINGS ARE IN ALL

---

[2] Ash's and Lake's *Frog Raising for Pleasure and Profit and Other Bizarre Books* (London: Macmillan, 1985), *Bizarre Books* (New York: St. Martin's, 1985; London: Sphere, 1987; London: Pavilion, 1998), *Fish Who Answer the Telephone and Other Bizarre Books* (London: Murray, 2006), *Bizarre Books: A Compendium of Classic Oddities* (New York: Perennial, 2007); Ash's *Potty, Fartwell, and Knob: From Luke Warm to Minty Badger — Extraordinary but True Names of British People* (London: Headline, 2007); Bell's *Scouts in Bondage and Other Violations of Literary Propriety* (New York: Simon and Schuster, 2007) and *Scouts in Bondage and Other Curious Works from Bygone Times with Titles that Might Cause Vulgar Minds to Misapprehend Their Content* (London: Aurum, 2006); and Ashmead's *Bertha Venation and Hundreds of Other Funny Names of Real People* (New York: HarperCollins; London: Profile, 2007).

CAPS, FOLLOWING OBSOLETE LIBRARY PRACTICE. [The Curator's comments are enclosed in square brackets.]

This book does not contain the entire list. In order to avoid offending or embarrassing anyone, I have omitted from the published version the names of any persons whom I know to be living. I apologize to anyone whom I may have offended or embarrassed, to those whom I incorrectly supposed were dead — and especially to any living authors with funny names who would have preferred to have been included.

The Inscribed List works best when it is read aloud in sequence. Try it in the staff lounge at lunch or coffee breaks, during lulls at conferences, while waiting for a quorum at staff meetings, or anywhere really, though perhaps not at job interviews.

With the publication of this book, I surrender my Curatorship to you, dear readers. Go for it!

Read on, librarians and non-librarians alike.

Use your imagination.

Laugh!

Out loud!

A dirty mind helps!

Abraham Jacob van der Aa (1792-1857)

Christianus Petrus Eliza Robidé van der Aa (1791-1851)

Pieter van der Aa (1659-1733)

Pierre Jean Baptiste Carel Robidé van der Aa (1832-1887)

Odd Abrahamsen (1924-2001)

Johann Erasmus Assmann, Freiherr von Abschatz (1646-1699)

Christos G. Aches (fl. 1952)

Psychology at Work (1932) by Lois Hayden Meek (b. 1894), edited by Paul Strong Achilles (b. 1890)

August Aichhorn (1878-1949)

Ax Ajax (fl. 1955)

Pavel Borisovich Aksel'rod (1850-1928)

Odd Per Leif Albert (b. 1896)

Sir Rutherford Alcock (1809-1897)

Zwy Aldouby (fl. 1971)

Prosper Alfaric (1876-1955)

Thomas Wildcat Alford (b. 1860)

T. Clifford Allbutt (1836-1925)

Harold John Allcock (fl. 1932)

Ruth Allcock (fl. 1943)

Sidney Allnutt (fl. 1910)

Wolf Aly (1881-1962)

Constancio Caga Amen (fl. 1958)

Alfred Anger (fl. 1958)

Harry Dell Anger (1888-1953)

Laura Angst (b. 1884)

H. Igor Ansoff (fl. 1957)

Anthropometry of Airline Stewardesses (1975)

August Antz (fl. 1930) [Worse than May flies or June bugs.]

Carl Caesar Antz (fl. 1836)

Eduard Ludwig Antz (fl. 1921)

François Anus (fl. 1934)

Pierre Anus (fl. 1977)

Anus Ma'ruf (fl. 1960)

István Apáthy (1829-1889)

Stefan Apáthy (fl. 1901)

Hippocrates George Apostle (fl. 1942)

"Aggressive Behavior of Nursery School Children and Adult Procedures in Dealing with Such Behavior" by Madeleine Hunt Appel (*Journal of Experimental Education*, 11 [December 1942]: 185-199)

Nils M. Apeland (fl. 1958)

Jules Aper (fl. 1881)

William Apes (b. 1798)

APES IN MOTION PICTURES

Rollo Appleyard (1867-1943)

Wanda Rector Arbuckle (fl. 1969)

Bill Arp (1826-1903)

Wart Arslan (fl. 1934)

Pierre Joseph Arson (fl. 1817)

Mosheh David Arson (fl. 1948)

Minimum Nets in Abstract Webs (1945) by
    Rafael Artzy

Boris Abramovich Ass (fl. 1960)

Josef Ass (b. 1910)

Edward Assbury (1904-1997)

Eugène Asse (1830-1901)

Fritz Asshoff (b. 1907)

Ernst Franz Gustav Assman (b. 1879)

Richard Assman (fl. 1924)

Christian Gottfried Assmann (1752-1822)

Ernst Assmann (d. 1926)

Richard Assmann (b. 1845)

Elmer Bugg Atwood (b. 1874)

Audefroi le Bastard (fl. 1200)

Peter Ax (b. 1927)

Machine Shop Mathematics (1951) by Aaron
    Axelrod

Walter Bäbbli (fl. 1949)

Wealthy Consuelo Babcock (fl. 1926)

Father Abraham (1925) by Irving Bacheller (1859-1950)

Ollie Lucy Backus (b. 1908)

Ernst Lecher Bacon (fl. 1917)

Friar Bacon (fl. 1828)

Pierre-Jean-Jacques Bacon-Tacon (1738-1817)

Mabel Annie Phillips Badcock (b. 1880)

Welbore St. Clair Baddeley (b. 1856)

Thomas Baddy (d. 1729)

George Badman (fl. 1960)

Halsey Joseph Bagg (b. 1889)

Henry Horneman Bagger (fl. 1923)

Holger Bagger (fl. 1900)

Sofus Bagger (fl. 1905)

Betty Cox Baggs (b. 1926)

Mae Lucy Baggs (fl. 1918)

Florence A. Baglehole (fl. 1873)

John Dryden Bags (fl. 1854)

Balint Bakfart (1507-1576)

Ruth Mae Morris Bakwin (b. 1898)

Bald's Leechbook (1955)

Ludwig von Baldass (1887-1963)

Robert Baldick (fl. 1955)

Sir Charles Bent Ball (1851-1916)

E.A.R. Ball (b. 1857?) [Usually published
    as Eustace Alfred Reynolds-Ball.]

Harry Ball (fl. 1929)

Mog Ball (fl. 1973)

Theodore Rolly Ball (b. 1883)

Wayland Dalrymple Ball (1858-1893)

Camillo Benso Ballabio (fl. 1972)

Albert V. Ballhatchet (fl. 1916) [Did he
    name an orchidectomy apparatus?]

Kenneth Ballhatchet (1922-1995)

Karl Joseph Napoleon Balling (1805-1868)

Ole Peter Hansen Balling (1823-1906)

Pieter Balling (fl. 1663)

Jens Christian Balling Engelsen (b. 1891)

Jacqueline Ballman (fl. 1969)

Electra Pearl Ballou (b. 1905)

Latimer Whipple Ballou (1812-1900)

Maturin Murray Ballou (1820-1895)

Arnold Kent Balls (b. 1891)

Josephine Balls (fl. 1958)

Lyman Balls (1898-1991)

Ruby Loosle Balls (fl. 1960)

William Lawrence Balls (1882-1960)

Edith Ballwebber (fl. 1933)

Gu Ban (32-92) [No goo allowed in China!]

Luisa Banal (b. 1895)

Wenceslau Polycarpo Banana (b. 1861)

Maharaja Bananathaji (fl. 1927)

Bernhard Laurits Frederik Bang (1848-1932)

Ivar Christian Bang (1869-1918)

Rebekka Hammering Bang (b. 1902)

Odd Bang-Hansen (fl. 1946)

Gay Esty Bangs (fl. 1899)

Mary Rogers Bangs (fl. 1910)

Outram Bangs (1862-1932)

BANGS FAMILY

Praisegod Barbon (1596?-1679)

Come Summer (1936) by Virginia McCarty Bare

Issachar Barebone (fl. 1753)

Devotions for Junior Highs (1960) by Helen F. Couch and Sam S. Barefield

Adelaide Pauline Barer (fl. 1931)

Shlomo Barer (b. 1919)

Joseph Michaël Thomas Barretto de Souza (1859-1940)

Barf Rut Men Gulāb (1979)

Henry E. Barff (fl. 1902)

Stafford E.D. Barff (fl. 1968)

Your Skin: An Owner's Guide (1995) by
Joseph P. Bark [Aha! That's why it's
so rough.]

Frank Stringfellow Barr (b. 1897)

Algernon Bastard (fl. 1903)

Thomas Bastard (1566-1618)

Natica Inches Bates (fl. 1917)

*The Golden Booke of the Leaden Goddes:
Wherein is Described the Vayne
Imaginations of Heathe Pagans, and
Counterfaict Christians, Wyth a
Description of Their Seueral Tables,
What Ech of Their Pictures Signified*
(1577) by Stephen Batman (d. 1584)

A.H.O.W. de Bats (fl. 1949)

Bernard Bats (fl. 1838)

Imbert de Bats (1670-1720)

Pierre de Bats (fl. 1700)

Franz Batsy (fl. 1909)

The Christian Mans Closet (1581) by
Barthélemy Batt (1515-1559) [Also
known as Bartholomaeus Battus,
Bartholomew Batty, and several
other variants.]

Max Batt (b. 1875)

Lelia McAnally Batte (b. 1887)

Constance de Rothschild Flower, Baroness Battersea (1843-1931)

A Treatise on Madness (1758) by William Battie (1704-1776)

Kemp Plummer Battle (1831-1919)

Hazel Lucile Wilson Battles (b. 1915)

Beatrice Stebbing Batty (fl. 1871)

Captain Robert Batty (d. 1848)

Espine Batty (fl. 1830)

W. de B.P. Batty-Smith (fl. 1871)

Edmund Ironside Bax (fl. 1891)

Pearce B. Ironside Bax (fl. 1900)

Batsell Barrett Baxter (b. 1916)

Ethnology of Pukapuka (1938) by Ernest Beaglehole (1906-1965) and Pearl Beaglehole (1910-1979)

John Cawte Beaglehole (1901-1971)

Byron Beans (fl. 1903)

George Harry Beans (b. 1894)

Leonardo List Beans (b. 1904)

Jack Beater (fl. 1959)

Robert Pierce Beaver (b. 1906)

Frigga Beetz (fl. 1936)

Wilhelm von Beetz (1822-1886)

Harry Beevers (b. 1904)

Lee Beggs (1871-1943)

The Behaviour of the Great Tit (1952)

Bozo Bek (fl. 1958)

Stanislaw Belch (1904-1989)

Supply Belcher (1751-1836)

Catharine Belches (fl. 1945)

Edward F. Belches (fl. 1939)

The Recipe Book of Herbs (1934) by Olive
Mills Belches

Eric Temple Bell (1883-1960)

Krista Bendová (fl. 1948)

The Benefit of Farting Explain'd (1720)

*The Benefit of Farting Farther Explain'd,
Vindicated, and Maintain'd, Against
Those Blunderbusses Who Will Not
Allow it to be Concordant to the
Cannon Law, Plainly Demonstrating,
that a Fart is In-Nose-Scent: that the
Use of it Will be of Great Come-Fart
to the People of Great Britain* (1720)

Lood van Bennekom (fl. 1953)

David Miles Bensusan-Butt (fl. 1960)

Arthur Cleveland Bent (1866-1954)

Sir John Poo Beresford (1766-1844)

Ernest Best (fl. 1955)

Nicolas Bidet, Seigneur de Juzancourt
(1702-1782)

Lee Bidgood (1884-1963)

The Origins of Christianity (1909) by
Charles Bigg (1840-1908) and
Thomas Banks Strong (1861-1944)

Thomas Plantagenet Bigg-Wither (1845-
1890)

Charles Robert Webster Biggar (1847-1909)

Leander Adams Bigger (b. 1844)

Millie Elizabeth Bigger (fl. 1910)

Ruby Vaughan Bigger (fl. 1924)

Urban Bigger (fl. 1911)

Maria Bigger-Bollschweiler (fl. 1939)

Earl Derr Biggers (1884-1933)

Kate Bighead (fl. 1933)

Stanley K. Bigman (fl. 1957)

Tarquinio Bignozzi (fl. 1941)

Alexandre Bigot, Baron de Monville (1607-
1675)

Marie Healy Bigot (b. 1843)

Vincent Bigot (1649-1720)

Sébastien François Bigot de Morogues
(1705-1781)

Queenie May Bilbo (fl. 1918)

In the Sky Garden (1922) by Stephen
Moylan Bird (1897-1919), edited by
Charles Wharton Stork (1881-1971)

George Lawrence Forsythe Birdsong (1821-
1869)

Gussie Mae Birdsong (fl. 1957)

Irene Belcher Birdsong (b. 1900)

McLemore Birdsong (b. 1911)

Ray Lee Birdwhistell (b. 1918)

Faber Birren (b. 1900)

George Birtwistle (fl. 1928)

Duck Keeping for Pleasure and Profit (1951)
      by Victor Birtwistle

David Skull Bispham (1857-1921)

Prophilla Chander Biswas (b. 1904)

Marcel Bitchy (fl. 1938)

Petr Mikhailovich Bitsilli (1879-1953)

Learner Blackman (1781?-1815)

Dust (1934) by Samuel Cyril Blacktin (b.
      1891)

Nash's Surgical Physiology (1953) by Brian
      Brewer Blades (b. 1906)

Harriot Stanton Blatch (1856-1940)

James Godson Bleak (1829-1918)

Leo Blech (1871-1958)

Claas Jouco Bleeker (b. 1898)

Walter Blith (fl. 1649)

Antonio Blitz (1810-1877)

*Nomenclature des oblitérations des timbres-
      postes français de 1849 à 1876*
      (1946) by Henry Blot (b. 1904)

Henri Georges Stephane Adolphe Opper de
    Blowitz (1825-1903)

Samuel Blows (fl. 1899)

Jasper Blowsnake (fl. 1914)

Sam Blowsnake (fl. 1920)

Andreas Blug (fl. 1932)

Lady Anne Blunt (1837-1917)

Betty Bacon Blunt (fl. 1940)

Stanhope English Blunt (1850-1926)

Wilfrid Scawen Blunt (1840-1922)

Judith Anne Dorothea Blunt-Lytton (b. 1873)

Burwell A. Bobo (fl. 1857)

Arlie Vernon Bock (b. 1888)

Péter Bod (1712-1769)

Temple Bodley (1852-1940)

Lukas Johann Boogers Böer (1751-1835)

Richard Constant Boer (1863-1929)

Francisco de Asís de Bofarull y Sans
    (1843-1936)

Conrad Humbert Boffa (b. 1913)

Lionel Frank Boffey (b. 1886)

Harriet Bog (fl. 1950)

Ingomar Bog (fl. 1956)

Rudolf Bog (fl. 1952)

Brackenbury Dickson Bogie (fl. 1843)

Boguphalus II, Bishop of Posen (fl. 1253)

Ottokar Bogus (fl. 1956)

Marg Alice Looney Bohn (fl. 1941)

Willy Boller (fl. 1957)

Léon Bollock (b. 1859)

Beverley Waugh Bond (b. 1881)

Edith Bone (fl. 1957)

Gertrude Helena Dodd, Lady Bone (b. 1876)

The Sex Life of Youth (1929) by Grace
    Loucks Elliott and Harry Bone

Sir Muirhead Bone (1876-1953)

Edoardo Giacomo Boner (1864-1908)

Ada Boni (fl. 1955)

Edgar Bonjour (b. 1898)

Heinrich Werner von Bonk (b. 1909)

Philippus Bonk (fl. 1738)

Wallace John Bonk (b. 1923)

Frances Bonker (fl. 1932)

Sigrid Boo (1898-1953)

Edouard Boob (fl. 1922)

Gustave Boob (fl. 1867)

William W. Boob (fl. 1890)

Nico Hendricus Johannes van den
    Boogaard (fl. 1974)

L.W. Boogerman (fl. 1920)

Gosuinus Hendricus Bernard van den Boom (fl. 1912)

Harm Boom (1810-1885)

Helmut Anton Wilhelm de Boor (b. 1891)

Ballington Booth (1859-1940)

Maud Ballington Booth (1865-1948)

Charlyne Ruth Booze (fl. 1954)

Stubborn Facts Concerning True Sexual Relations (1876) by H.W. Boozer

C.D. Bopp (b. 1923)

Gustavo Bopp Blu (fl. 1948)

Joseph B. Bopp (fl. 1978)

Johann Boppenhausen (ca. 1666-1740)

Eleanor Bor (fl. 1952)

Otto Frederik Christian William Borchsenius (1844-1925)

Omen Konn Boring (fl. 1929)

The Boring Ctenostomate Bryozoa: Taxonomy and Paleobiology Based on Cavities in Calcareous Substrata (1978)

BORING FAMILY

The Boring Mechanism of Teredo (1924)

Thomas David Boslooper (b. 1923)

Henry Rush Boss (b. 1835)

Edward Increase Bosworth (1861-1927)

Charles Marie Joseph Bra (fl. 1895)

Felix de Bra (b. 1879)

Giuseppe da Bra (b. 1884)

Hendrik van Bra (b. 1555)

Kurt de Bra (fl. 1913)

Mabel de Bra (fl. 1929)

Théophile Bra (fl. 1827)

Vittorio Murari Brà (fl. 1923)

Abraham Chaim Braatbard (1699-1786)

Wallop Brabazon (fl. 1848)

Anne Bracegirdle (ca. 1663-1748)

Brian Bracegirdle (fl. 1971)

William Frederick Braggs (b. 1892)

Recent Advances in Neurology (1929),
    Diseases of the Nervous System
    (1933), "Some Reflections on
    Genius" (1948), *Mind, Perception,
    and Science* (1951), and *The
    Contribution of Medicine to Our Idea
    of the Mind* (1952), all by W. Russell
    Brain, Baron Brain (1895-1966)

Annie Allnutt, Baroness Brassey (1839-
    1887)

Leo Brat (b. 1910)

Mary Agnes Burniston Brazier (b. 1904)

James Henry Breasted (1865-1935)

Sophonisba Preston Breckinridge (1866-
    1948)

The Breeding Biology of the Blue-Faced Booby (1968)

Quirinus Breen (b. 1896)

John Seargeant Cyprian Bridge (fl. 1921)

Selwyn John Curwen Brinton (1859-1940)

Garland Carr Broadhead (1827-1912)

Natalie Bruck-Auffenberg (b. 1877)

Ada M. Zimmerman Brunk (1908-1954)

John Stubbs Brushwood (1920-2007)

Handasyde Buchanan (fl. 1962)

Carl Darling Buck (1866-1955) [Oh, please do! Cf. Walter Flex.]

Pearl Sydenstricker Buck (1892-1973)

Kyr Ivan Bucko (fl. 1949)

Buddhists and Glaciers of Western Tibet (1933)

Sir Ernest Alfred Wallis Budge (1857-1934)

Thea Budnick (fl. 1934)

Buffalo Child Long Lance (1890-1932)

Neal Dollison Buffaloe (b. 1924)

Imbrie Buffum (b. 1915)

Edwin Holmes Bugbee (1820-1900)

Bertha Warden Bugg (fl. 1957)

Charles O'Kelly Bugg (1902-1980)

Dailey Leo Bugg (fl. 1929)

Francis Bugg (1640-1724?)

James Luckin Bugg (b. 1920)

Leila Hardin Bugg (fl. 1905)

Mary Cobb Bugg (fl. 1958)

Sterling Lowe Bugg (fl. 1955)

William Emmanuel Bugg (1848-1935)

BUGG FAMILY

Astrid Scholdager Bugge (b. 1902)

Kathrina Van Wagenen Bugge (fl. 1927)

Erich Arnold von Buggenhagen (fl. 1951)

Friedrich Bügger (fl. 1917)

JoAnne Buggey (fl. 1960)

Edvard Hagerup Bull (1855-1938)

Ludlow Seguine Bull (1886-1954)

Ole Bull (1810-1880)

Principles of Feeding Farm Animals (1916),
*Effects of Sex, Length of Feeding
Period, and a Ration of Ear-Corn
Silage on the Quality of Baby Beef*
(1930), *The Effect of Pregnancy on
the Quality of Beef* (1944), *Beef for
the Table* (1944), *Veal for the Table*
(1948), and *Meat for the Table* (1951),
all by Sleeter Bull (b. 1887)

Anton Bum (1856-1925)

Charles Weathers Bump (1872-1908) [He
is tough.]

Thomas Francis Bumpus (1861-1916)

Günther Bung (fl. 1937)

Bungee Jumping for Fun and Profit (1992)

Rev. Albert Carrier Bunn (fl. 1902)

Clinton Orrin Bunn (b. 1877)

Romanzo Bunn (1829-1909)

Romanzo Norton Bunn (fl. 1928)

The Whole Summe of Christian Religion
(1576) by Edmund Bunny
[presumably includes Easter]

Benedictus Buns (1642-1716)

Elmer Henry Buns (fl. 1935)

Johann Hermann Buns (b. 1898)

The Glorious Dead (1919) by Bishop
Herbert Bury (1853-1933)

Reynaldo Kuntz Busch (fl. 1967)

Harry J. Bush (b. 1880)

Harry R. Bush (fl. 1954)

Harry V. Bush (fl. 1938)

Kate Buss (fl. 1930)

Fanny Butcher (1888-1987)

Charlotte Wimp Butler (fl. 1917)

Albert Fidelis Butsch (fl. 1876)

The Anatomy of the Labrador Duck (1958)
by Philip Strong Humphrey (b. 1926)
and Robert Stearns Butsch (b. 1914)
[That's one tough duck!]

Russell Lewis Carl Butsch (b. 1897)

Archibald Willingham Butt (1866-1912)

Edmund Dargan Butt (b. 1898)

Newbern Isaac Butt (fl. 1925)

Frederick William Butt-Thompson (fl. 1952)

Christopher Hendrik Dirk Buys Ballot
    (1817-1890)

Harry Lood Byrd (1887-1966)

Ingram Bywater (1840-1914)

Leroy Cabbage (fl. 1940)

Charles-Louis Cadet de Gassicourt (1769-
    1821)

North Callahan (1908-2004)

Northern J. Calloway (fl. 1977)

Sicko van Camminga (fl. 1622)

LeGrand Cannon (b. 1899)

Madeleine Carabo-Cone (b. 1916)

Bukk G. Carleton (1856-1914)

Bliss Carman (1861-1929)

Clark Clements Carnal (b. 1914)

Marguerite Carnal (b. 1899)

Effie May Carp (fl. 1921)

Eugène Antoine Désiré Émile Carp (1895-1983)

Frances Merchant Carp (b. 1918)

Horia Carp (1869-1943)

Teresa Carpenter Carp (fl. 1972)

J. Carp-Coox (fl. 1767)

Eskimo Realities (1973) by Edmund Snow Carpenter

The Windward Road (1956) by Archie Fairly Carr (1909-1987)

Donald Eaton Carr (b. 1903) [Yummy!]

John Beans Carrell (1851-1950)

Robert Looney Caruthers (1800-1882)

Lavender Cassels (b. 1916)

Waddill Catchings (b. 1879)

The Cement Fuck (1966)

French Ensor Chadwick (1844-1919)

Chasing Gold for Fun and Profit (1981)

Atlas Lawrence Cheek (fl. 1937)

Sir Louis Chick (fl. 1953)

Ralph Chick Chick (fl. 1952) [sic]

John George Children (1777-1852)

T.R. Chintamani Dikshit (fl. 1929)

Max Chop (1862-1929)

Yu Chu (fl. 1943)

Bholanauth Chunder (b. 1822)

Pratap Chandra Chunder (b. 1919)

William Farr Church (b. 1912)

Fleetwood Churchill (1808-1878)

William Crumby Claghorn (b. 1875)

Helen B. Clapesattle (b. 1908)

Edward Bull Clapp (1856-1919)

Gordon Rufus Clapp (1905-1963)

The History of the Microscope (1932) by
Reginald Stanley Clay and Thomas
H. Court [Why didn't they write
about tennis?]

*Clean Asshole Poems and Smiling Vegetable
Songs* (1978)

Paul Adolphe van Cleemputte (1837-1916)

Victor Clinton Clinton-Baddeley (1900-1970)

Edward Clodd (1840-1930)

Antoine Barthélémy Clot (1793-1868)

Suzanne Clot (fl. 1914)

Charles Clutterbuck (b. 1755)

Cuthbert Clutterbuck of Kennaquhair (fl.
1836)

Henry Clutterbuck (1767-1856)

*What Shall We Have for Dinner?: Satis-
factorily Answered by Numerous
Bills of Fare for from Two to Eighteen*

Persons (1852) by Lady Maria Clutterbuck [pseudonym of Catherine
Thomson Dickens (1815-1879)]

Lewis Augustus Clutterbuck (b. 1854)

Medwin Caspar Clutterbuck (b. 1865)

Robert Hawley Clutterbuck (1837-1896)

Raymond de Coccola (b. 1912)

Adolf Marie de Cock (fl. 1862)

Alfons de Cock (1850-1921)

Conrad Cock (fl. 1778)

Gerardus Johannes Theodorus Maria Cock
(fl. 1947)

Helenius de Cock (1824-1895)

Hendrik de Cock (1801-1842)

Hieronymus Cock (ca. 1510-1570)

I.C. de Cock (fl. 1905)

*Simple Strains: or, The Homespun Lays of
an Untutored Muse* (1806) by James
Cock (b. 1752)

Jan Kornelis de Cock (1867-1941)

Maurice de Cock (fl. 1912)

Max de Cock (fl. 1941)

Oliver Jeste Cock (fl. 1956)

Theodorus Balthasar de Cock (1650-1720)

Victor Cock (fl. 1933)

William Hendy Cock (b. 1873)

Alfredo Cock Arango (1894-1965)

Emilie de Cock Buning (fl. 1936)

Lucia Cock de Bernal Jimenez (fl. 1957)

Julián Cock Escobar (fl. 1950)

COCK FAMILY

The Symptoms, Nature, Cause, and Cure of a Gonorrhoea (1713) by William Cockburn (1669-1739)

COCKE FAMILY

Charles T. Cockey (fl. 1885)

Frederick Seymour Cocks (b. 1882)

Orrin Giddings Cocks (b. 1877)

John Vincent Cockshoot (b. 1924)

A.O.J. Cockshut (fl. 1955)

Herman Joseph Bond Cockshutt (b. 1907)

Ignatius Cockshutt (1812-1901)

Nevill Coghill (b. 1899)

Sir Aston Cokayne (1608-1684)

The Gentlewoman at Home (1892) by Charlotte Talbot Coke

Dorothea Prance Coke (b. 1884)

Sir Edward Coke (1552-1634)

Audrey Butt Colson (fl. 1953)

The Complete Anas of Thomas Jefferson (1903) [Will the sequel be *The Complete Rectam of James Madison*?]

Paul Condom (fl. 1925)

Cemil Conk (b. 1873)

Ellsworth Prouty Conkle (fl. 1938)

Leslie J. Cookenboo (fl. 1955)

Benjamin Franklin Cooling (b. 1938)

Mary Elizabeth Cooling (fl. 1954)

Wilmer Colebrook Cooling (b. 1921)

Dotia Trigg Cooney (fl. 1911)

Sir Colin Reith Coote (b. 1893)

Charles Over Cornelius (1890-1937) [When
        will Cornelius get a turn to be on top?
        Cf. Walter Balls Headley.]

Albert Charles Cornsweet (fl. 1939)

Douglas Cow (fl. 1920)

James Cow (1854-1923)

John Cow (fl. 1841)

Raymond Gibson Cowherd (b. 1910)

Althea Brinckerhoff Crawford Cox (1852-
        1909)

David Roxbee Cox (fl. 1958)

Harold Roxbee Cox, Baron Kings Norton (b.
        1902)

Harry Cox (b. 1923)

Homersham Cox (1821-1897)

Hyde Cox (fl. 1966) [Yes, one should
        always be modest.]

The Gentlemans Recreation (1928) by Nicholas Cox, preface by E.D. Cuming

Ulysses Orange Cox (b. 1864)

Owen Cockran Coy (b. 1884)

Walter Crack (fl. 1901)

Hubert Crackanthorpe (1870-1896)

Montague Crackanthorpe (1832-1913)

Cecil Van Meter Crabb (b. 1889)

Dinah Maria Mulock Craik (1826-1887)

Ralph Adams Cram (1863-1942)

John Colet, the Prophet Dean of St. Pauls (1907) by Katherine Priest Crank

John Cranko (fl. 1957)

Charles F. Crap (b. ca. 1828)

Camille Charles Craplet (b. 1920)

Chanoine Bernard Craplet (fl. 1958)

The Story of William Wallace Crapo, 1830-1926 (1942) by Henry Howland Crapo (b. 1862)

Edith Bertha Crapper (fl. 1893)

Ellis H. Crapper (fl. 1907)

John Craps (fl. 1856)

Adelaide Crapsey (1878-1914)

Algernon Sidney Crapsey (1847-1927)

Basil Long Crapster (fl. 1949)

CREATIVE ACTIVITIES AND SEAT WORK

Evelyn Baring of Cromer (fl. 1908)

The Anglican Episcopate and the American Colonies (1902) by Arthur Lyon Cross (1873-1940)

Walter John Blyth Crotch (fl. 1928)

Elie-Victor-Benjamin, Baron Crud (1772-1845)

Bartley Cavanaugh Crum (1900-1959)

Earl Le Verne Crum (1891-1961)

Gertrude Bosworth Crum (fl. 1938)

Josie Moore Crum (fl. 1957)

Mason Crum (b. 1887)

Ralph Brinckerhoff Crum (b. 1888)

Samuel Ebb Crumb (b. 1880)

Calvin Crumbaker (b. 1885)

Alexander Crumby (fl. 1690)

Robert O. Crummey (fl. 1959)

Lucy Hill Crump (fl. 1926)

Norman Easedale Crump (b. 1896)

Richard Burton Cuddleback (b. 1922)

William Herman Cuddleback (1852-1919)

William Louis Cuddleback (b. 1854)

Mari Anus Cuming (b. 1845)

Primrose Cumming (1915-2004)

P. Cuntaram Pillai (1855-1897)

Ivan Cunt (fl. 1968)

Adeline Cunti (fl. 1942)

Mozart de Cunto (fl. 1950)

Heinrich Cuntz (b. 1873)

Johannes H. Cuntz (fl. 1892)

Otto Cuntz (1865-1932)

Ferdinand de Cornot, Baron de Cussy (1795-1866)

Anna Maria Elizabeth Cust (fl. 1902)

Thomas Darl Cutsforth (b. 1893)

Landmarks in Surgical Progress (1928-1929) and *Surgery of the Century, 1830-1930* (1930), both by Irving Samuel Cutter (1875-1945)

CUTTHROAT TROUT

Bozo Cvjetkovic (1879-1952)

Irene Briggs DaBoll (fl. 1969)

Titt Fasmer Dahl (b. 1903)

Conditioning for Distance Running (1978) by Jack Daniels (b. 1933)

Wheeler Padlar Davey (b. 1886)

Philip Heckle Davidson (fl. 1937)

John A. Day (fl. 1961) [You can't make a living as a prostitute at that rate.]

Matthew Paul Deady (1824-1893) [He should have done an edition of Livy.]

DEATH — COLLECTIONS

Desiree De Charms (fl. 1953)

Noël Deerr (b. 1874)

Karl Deichgräber (b. 1903)

Floy Winks Delancey (fl. 1960)

Mayhew Derryberry (b. 1902)

Guido van Deth (1913-1969)

William Potts Dewees (1768-1841)

Thomas Cockey Deye (ca. 1728-1807)

Harry Richard Dick (fl. 1953)

A Survey of Humanistic Work in Progress on the Pacific Coast, 1945-46 (1947) by Hugh G. Dick (b. 1909)

Isaac Meir Dick (1814-1893)

Jack R. Dick (fl. 1973?)

DICK FAMILY

Forrest Dicks (b. 1900)

Joke Dijkshoorn (fl. 1951)

Ahmad Amin Dik (fl. 1902)

Cor Dik (fl. 1959)

Slavko S. Diklic (fl. 1932)

Mathura Prasada Dikshit (1878-1966)

Emilia Francis Strong, Lady Dilke (1840-1904)

Oswald Ashton Wentworth Dilke (fl. 1954)

Arthur Urbane Dilley (b. 1873)

Ling Ding (b. 1904)

You Ding (fl. 1958)

Aylward Edward Dingle (b. 1874)

Herbert Dingle (b. 1890)

Reginald James Dingle (b. 1889)

Raymond C. Dingledine (fl. 1959)

Amasa Dingley (d. 1798)

Eric John Dingwall (fl. 1957)

Berhanu Dinke (fl. 1950)

Picturesque English Cottages and Their Doorway Gardens (1905) by Peter Hampson Ditchfield (1854-1930)

Beulah Marie Dix (1876-1970)

Ernest Reginald McClintock Dix (1857-1936)

Father Gregory Dix (fl. 1945)

John Adams Dix (1798-1879)

Lester Dix (b. 1890)

Morgan Dix (1827-1908)

Otto Dix (1891-1969)

Elliott Van Kirk Dobbie (b. 1907)

Elithe Outlaw Doby (fl. 1950)

C.C. Doctor (b. 1925)

Willem Emile Théodore Marie van der Does de Willebois (fl. 1892)

Edgar Arnold Doll (b. 1889)

John Syng Dorsey (1783-1818)

Wilfrid Hogarth Dowdeswell (fl. 1960)

Henry Sandwith Drinker (1880-1965)

Introduction to Anesthesia (1949) by Robert Dunning Dripps (1911-1973)

Godfrey Rolles Driver (1892-1975) [Godfrey oppresses the lower class.]

Rev. Samuel Rolles Driver (1846-1914) [It seems that a tendency to oppressing the lower class runs in the family.]

Marie Luise Droop (fl. 1934)

Sir Arthur Duck (1580-1648)

Plastics and Rubbers (1971) by Edward William Duck

Arnold Duckwitz (1802-1881) [He's every bit as smart as a duck!]

Henri La Fayette Villaume Ducoudray Holstein (1763-1839)

Max Dude (fl. 1903)

Wim Duk (fl. 1945)

Charles Elwood Dull (1878-1947)

Raymond William Dull (1874-1948)

Lee D. Dumm (fl. 1960) [♫ dum dee dee ♫]

Robert Dennis Dumm (fl. 1933)

Sebastian Cabot Dumm (fl. 1872)

Anthony C. Dumper (fl. 1953)

Bi Dung (b. 1909) [On sale! Cheap! Makes
    great fertilizer!]

Dorothy I.Y. Dung (fl. 1953)

Jerzy Sewer Dunin-Borkowski (1856-1908)

Edward John Moreton Drax Plunkett,
    Baron Dunsany (1878-1957)

Antoine Amédée Du Paty de Clam (1813-
    1887)

Romesh Chunder Dutt (1848-1909)

Erminius Stanislaus Duzy (b. 1915)

DWARF STARS — CONGRESSES

William Addison Dwiggins (1880-1956)

Doris Dyke (b. 1930)

Wilma Dykeman (fl. 1955)

*EPA Experiences in Oxygen-Activated
    Sludge* (1974)

Jubal Anderson Early (1816-1894)

Ernest Penney Earnest (b. 1901)

Allen Hendershott Eaton (b. 1878)

Edwin Butt Eckel (b. 1906)

Wealthy Rowena Edgerton (b. 1840)

Dirk van Eek (b. 1871)

Hilding Eek (b. 1910)

Sven Eek (b. 1900)

Claas Eel (fl. 1768)

Roeloff Eelbo (b. ca. 1733)

Walter Crosby Eells (1886-1962)

Elon Eels (fl. 1911)

Fritz Egg (fl. 1931)

Lois Egg (1913-1999)

Matthew H. Elbow (fl. 1953)

Peter Elbow (fl. 1953)

Adriana Elephant (b. 1911)

Taslim Olawale Elias (fl. 1956)

Gerald Frank Else (b. 1908)

The Neverending Story (1983) by Michael
    Ende

Berenice Apes Endler (fl. 1978)

Earl J. Ends (fl. 1959)

Speedy Eric (fl. 1960)

Thomas Hay Sweet Escott (1844-1924)

Jumbo Saul Etuk-Udo (fl. 1960)

Edwin Othello Excell (1851-1921)

Exploiting Your Company for Fun and Profit
    (1981)

Fulvia de Cunto Fadigas (fl. 1962)

William Buller Fagg (fl. 1953)

Hermann Fäh (fl. 1913)

Fake (1893-1972)

Guy Leverne Fake (fl. 1943)

Kenneth H. Fake (fl. 1937)

FAKE FAMILY

Arthur Spenser Loat Farquharson (1871-1942)

Finis King Farr (fl. 1911)

Negley Farson (1890-1960)

A.J. Farto (fl. 1954)

Novice G. Fawcett (b. 1909)

Best Friend (1977) by Pat Feeley

Rendigs Fels (b. 1917)

Vergilius Ture Anselm Ferm (1896-1974)

Fanny Fern (1811-1872)

Sir Arthur Frederic Brownlow Fforde (fl. 1947)

Yvonne Ffrench (fl. 1938)

Frederick Augustus Fidfaddy (fl. 1816)

Blasius Fimpel (fl. 1603)

Ludwig Fimpel (fl. 1942)

Zera Silver Fink (b. 1902)

Ina Ten Eyck Firkins (1866-1937)

The Necessity of Deepening the Mouth of the Mississippi River (1900) by Stuyvesant Fish (1851-1923)

Louise Bang Fisher (b. 1886)

Edward Fitzball (1792-1873)

William Shoemaker Flash (fl. 1954)

Jack Flasher (fl. 1947)

J. Froude Flashman (fl. 1908)

Paul Flat (1865-1918)

Károly Flatt Alföldi (1853-1905)

Sir Antony Garrard Newton Flew (b. 1923)

Walter Flex (1887-1917) [A name in the form of an imperative. Cf. Carl Darling Buck.]

Fred Morrow Fling (1860-1934)

John Ehret Flitcroft (fl. 1929)

Benjamin Orange Flower (1858-1918)

Gorch Fock (1880-1916)

Dingle Foot (b. 1905)

Joke Forceville - Van Rossum (b. 1927)

Lawson Forfeitt (fl. 1908)

Madame Jeanne Justine Fouqueau de Pussy (1786-1864)

Frank Fowell (fl. 1913)

Frank Bird Fox (b. 1876)

The Hunter Out of Time (1965) by Gardner
    Francis Fox (1911-1986)

John Joshua Quick Fox (fl. 1969)

Frameworks for Dating Fossil Man (1964)
    [Wouldn't you do better just to stay
    home alone for the evening?]

Albert Frigg (fl. 1953)

Onofrio Friggio (fl. 17th century)

Stephen Hole Fritchman (b. 1902)

John Frogg (fl. 1747)

Frogs for Fun and Profit? (ca. 1980?)

Lili Fröhlich-Bum (fl. 1924)

Tillie Badu Moss Fry (b. 1914)

Johann Fück (1894-1974)

Fuck You: A Magazine of the Arts (1962-
    1965)

Friedrich Jacob Fucker (fl. 1777)

Heinz Fucker (b. 1913)

Gertrud Fucker (fl. 1925)

H. Fukkink (fl. 1941)

Aleksandra Andreevna Fuks (1805-1883)

Alexander Fuks (b. 1917)

Aron Abramovich Fuks (fl. 1951)

Boris Abramovich Fuks (fl. 1959)

Boris Borisovich Fuks (fl. 1959)

Karl Fedorovich Fuks (1776-1846)

Lajb Fuks (b. 1908)

Svatomir Fuks (fl. 1944)

Tanya Fuks (fl. 1947)

Ulpian Fulwell (fl. 1586)

Karl Wilhelm Ferdinand von Funck (1761-1828)

Clotilde Embree Funk (fl. 1952)

Tamás Füssy (fl. 1902)

Opal Futch (fl. 1941)

Ovid L. Futch (fl. 1959)

Johann Joseph Fux (1660-1741)

Flavia Gág (b. 1907)

Millions of Cats (1928), *The Funny Thing* (1929), *Snippy and Snappy* (1931), *Nothing at All* (1941), and *Three Gay Tales from Grimm* (1943) all by Wanda Gág (1893-1946)

Anonymus Gallus (1066-1145)

Gamma Rays for Fun and Profit (1966)

Catherine Henrietta Wallop Milnes, Lady Gaskell (fl. 1919)

Sherlock Bronson Gass (1878-1945)

Harvey M. Gayman (fl. 1911) [Outed at
birth!]

Robert Tittermary Gebler (b. 1889)

A.C. Geekie (fl. 1871)

George Geekie (fl. 1923)

Edith Gerson-Kiwi (fl. 1937)

Esther Gerson-Kiwi (fl. 1955)

*Getting Along With the Chinese for Fun and
Profit* (1998)

Lenore Kramp Geweke (fl. 1930)

The Waterlover's Guide to Marine Medicine
(1993) by Paul G. Gill

*Catalogue of the Fishes of the East Coast of
North America* (1873), *A Remarkable
Genus of Fishes: The Umbras* (1904),
*The Tarpon and Lady-Fish and Their
Relatives* (1907), *The Archer-Fish
and Its Feats* (1910), and *The Story
of the Devil-Fish* (1910), all by
Theodore Gill (1837-1914)

Gathorne Robert Girdlestone (1881-1950)

Joan Bourne Glad (fl. 1960)

Clyde Chew Glascock (b. 1872)

Comstock Glaser (fl. 1935)

John Bruce Glassburner (b. 1920)

George Parkin de Twenebroker Glazebrook
(b. 1899)

Peter Vilhelm Glob (b. 1911)

Margaret Schleef Glock (fl. 1955)

Sir John Bagot Glubb (1897-1986)

Ludwig Glutting (fl. 1949)

Robert Glutz-Blotzheim (1786-1818)

Albrecht Goes (b. 1908) [Where?]

Brison Dowling Gooch (b. 1925)

George Peabody Gooch (1873-1968)

Ward Hunt Goodenough (fl. 1953)

The Goodpastures of Iowa and Washington, with Related Families (Tribbles, Osbornes & Bidlakes) (1971) by Robert Abraham Goodpasture (b. 1909)

Alfred Thomas Scrope Goodrick (b. 1857)

Bess Goodykoontz (1894-1990)

Colin Brummitt Goodykoontz (1885-1958)

Wouter van Gool (fl. 1953)

Karl Friedrich Sophus Goose (b. 1839)

George Hatfield Dingley Gossip (fl. 1891)

The Goose is Out (1956) by William John Grabb

Jane Bissell Grabhorn (1911-1973)

John Temple Graves (1856-1925)

Poems of Simplicity: and, The Living Dead (1938) by Linwood D. Graves

Roger Winks Gray (fl. 1947)

Adwin Wigfall Green (b. 1900)

Samuel Swett Green (1837-1918)

Jack P. Greene (fl. 1959)

Welcome Arnold Greene (1795-1870)

Emerson Frank Greenman (b. 1895)

Roy Orval Greep (b. 1905)

Egbert Grim (b. 1605)

Arthur Grime (fl. 1936)

Muriel Grindrod (fl. 1955)

Cocaine: A Drug and its Social Evolution (1976) by Lester Grinspoon

Sybren Ruurds de Groot (b. 1916)

Wolf-Dietrich Grope (fl. 1950)

Fritz Gropengiesser (fl. 1939)

August Wilhelm Hermann Gropengiesser (b. 1879)

Jacob Ashel Groper (1890-1966)

Fanny A. Gross (fl. 1944)

Growing Earthworms for Fun and Profit (1974)

Sir Kenneth George Grubb (fl. 1927)

C.T. Studd: Cricketer and Pioneer (1933), *After C.T. Studd* (1946), and *C.T. Studd: Athlete and Pioneer* (1947), all by Norman Percy Grubb (b. 1895)

Agostino Antonio Grubbissich (fl. 1869)

Henry Alexander Grubbs (b. 1904)

Aleksandr Ianovich Grunt (fl. 1960)

Ian Ianovich Grunt (fl. 1927)

Ottokar Grunt (fl. 1913)

Valentin Gruntz (fl. 1639)

A Guide to Sexing Chicks (1935)

Caroline Snowden Whitmarsh Guild (1827-1898)

Cyril Arthur Edward Ranger Gull (1876-1923)

Richard Gump (1906-1989)

Ludwig Gumplowicz (1838-1909)

Gunrunning for Fun and Profit (1986)

Wai-Wai: Through the Forests North of the Amazon (1958) by Nicholas Guppy (fl. 1958) [Why indeed!]

Edward Tisdale Gushée (b. 1896)

Albert Gut (1883-1947)

Arnoldo Nicolau de Flue Gut (b. 1895)

Fritz Gut (fl. 1944)

Gottlieb Gut (b. 1912)

Max Gut (b. 1877)

Max Gut (b. 1898)

Erwin Anton Gutkind (1886-1968)

Kurt Sigmar Gutkind (b. 1896)

Johann Christoph Friedrich Guts Muths (1759-1839)

Henry Rider Haggard (1856-1925)

Gove Hambidge (b. 1890)

Learned Hand (1872-1961)

*Handling Manure in the Deep-Pit Cage
    Laying-House* (1976)

Kathryn Trimmer Abbey Hanna (b. 1895)

Bent Hansen (b. 1920)

Sir Roger Hog, Lord Harcarse (1635?-1700)

Margaret Steel Hard (fl. 1936)

Walter R. Hard (b. 1882)

James Aloysius, Baron Harden-Hickey
    (1854-1898)

Paul O. Harder (fl. 1954)

The Theory of Presupposition Failure (1976)
    by Peter Harder and Christian Kock

Harm Harms (fl. 1940)

Pauline Titus Harms (fl. 1940)

Hastings Hornell Hart (1851-1932)

Lewis J. Hash (fl. 1951)

Margaret Masson Hardie Hasluck (1885-
    1948)

Hudson Bridge Hastings (fl. 1923)

Harlan Henthorne Hatcher (b. 1898)

Violet Sweet Haven (fl. 1940)

Siwart Haverkamp (1684-1742)

Sara Mae Stinchfield Hawk (b. 1885)

John Newbold Hazard (b. 1909)

Walter Balls Headley (1842-1918) [When will Headley get to ball Walter? Cf. Charles Over Cornelius.]

Edmund Markham Heale, M.A., Rector of Yelling, near Huntingdon (fl. 1863)

Gwinn Harris Heap (1817-1887)

Oliver Heaviside (1850-1925)

Bertha Yell Hebb (fl. 1922)

Fenwick Yellowley Hedley (fl. 1884)

Luella Vig Hefty (fl. 1973)

Donald W. Heiney (fl. 1954)

Helmut Hell (fl. 1960)

Hildegard Hell (b. 1903)

Miksa Hell (1720-1792)

Vera Hell (fl. 1960)

Willem Frederik van Hell (fl. 1931)

Ernest Hello (1828-1885)

Sir Arthur Helps (1813-1875)

M. Butt Hewson (fl. 1876)

Stanley High (1895-1961)

Frank Alpine Hill (1841-1901)

James Inches Hillocks (1826-1872)

Fred Junkin Hinkhouse (b. 1895)

Edwin James Hipkiss (1885-1955)

Worm Hirsch (b. 1902)

Eric C. Hiscock (fl. 1956)

Richard Hiscocks (fl. 1957)

Codman Hislop (fl. 1940)

G.W. Hitman (fl. 1960)

Grace Ping-Poo Ho (fl. 1960)

George Frisbie Hoar (1826-1904)

Leonard Trelawney Hobhouse (1864-1929)

Mogens Høg (1593-1661) [Cf. Gregers
      Krabbe.]

William Hog (b. ca. 1652)

Lancelot Thomas Hogben (1895-1975)

Herbert Ian Hogbin (1904-1989)

Hope W. Hogg (1863-1912)

James Hogg (1770-1835)

Margaret Hope Hogg (b. 1894)

Vasyl' Panasovych Hohol' (1777-1825)

Odd Hølaas (1898-1968)

Alexander Holder-Barell (fl. 1959)

English Sports and Pastimes (1949) by
      Christina Hole (1896-1985)

Frank Binford Hole (b. 1874)

Byron Sharpe Hollinshead (b. 1901)

Henderson Looney Holman, Jr. (1903-1967)

Urban Tigner Holmes (b. 1900)

Adèle Hommaire de Hell (1815?-1883?)

Xavier Hommaire de Hell (1812-1848)

Léon Pol Homo (1872-1957)

Sir de Symons Montagu George Honey
(1872-1945)

John Raymond de Symons Honey (fl. 1970)

Reginald Crawshaw Honeybone (fl. 1958)

Abraham Van Doren Honeyman (1849-1936)

Icie Gertrude Macy Hoobler (b. 1892)

Egbert van den Hoof (fl. 1655)

Sister David Hopfinger (fl. 1924)

Gunnar Hoppe (b. 1914)

*History of the Hopping Family in England
and Genealogy of the John Hopping
Family in America* (1952) by Edward
Stuart Hopping (b. 1871) and Louis
M. Hopping (b. 1900) [Is john hop-
ping similar to bar hopping?]

HOPPING FAMILY

Tom Hops (1906-1976)

Helmut Hör (fl. 1960)

Isaline Blew Horner (1896-1981)

*The Overvaluation of Love: A Study of a
Common Present-Day Feminine Type*
(1934) by Karen Horney (1885-1952)

Isabel Katherine Hornibrook (b. 1859)

Hugo Horny (b. 1881)

Dolores Jane Hornyak (fl. 1960)

George P. Horse Capture (fl. 1976)

HORSEMEN AND HORSEWOMEN [Not
centaurs?]

Outerbridge Horsey (1777-1842)

George Washington Hoss (1824-1906)

Kate Hotblack (fl. 1917)

François Hotman (1524-1590)

Leslie Hotson (b. 1897)

George P. Hott (fl. 1900)

Marie Donald Mackie Hottinger (b. 1893)

Julius Temple House (fl. 1924)

Roy Temple House (b. 1878)

House-Flipping for Fun and Profit (1997)

How I Became a Freak (1998)

How I Became a Holy Mother (1976)

How I Became Stupid (2004)

How to Abandon Ship (1942)

How to Abduct a Highland Lord (2007)

How to Achieve the Inevitable (1943)

How to Attract the Wombat (1949)

How to Avoid Huge Ships (1993)

*How to Avoid Intercourse With Your
Unfriendly Car Mechanic* (1977)

How to Avoid the Evil Eye (1985)

How to Be a Bad Singer (1989)

How to Be a Bitch With Style (1998)

How to Be a Domestic Goddess (2000)

How to Be a Failure (1970)

How to Be a Gate-Crasher (1929)

How to Be a Genius (1916)

How to Be a Ghost Hunter (2003)

How to Be a Ham (1981)

How to Be a Happy Cat (1987)

How to Be a Hermit (1929)

How to Be a Hero (1968)

How to Be a Little Mermaid (1998)

How to Be a Lousy Secretary (1976)

How to Be a Medieval Knight (2005)

How to Be a Megalomaniac (2002)

How to Be a Nonconformist (1967)

How to Be a Party Girl (1968)

How to Be a Perfect Bitch (1983)

How to Be a Perfect Person in Just Three Days (1984)

How to Be a Perfect Princess (2006)

How to Be a Perfect Stranger (1996)

How to Be a Pig (2002)

How to Be a Pirate (2005)

How to Be a Polite Jerk (2007)

How to Be a Rich Nigger (1979)

How to Be a Roman Soldier (2005)

How to Be a Saint: Made Simple for Busy People (1987)

How to Be a Samurai Warrior (2005)

How to Be a Sex Goddess (2005)

How to Be a Sex Rascal (1997)

How to Be a Sincere Phoney (1999)

How to Be a Successful Dog (1999)

How to Be Alone (2002)

How to Be an Ocean Scientist in Your Own Home (1988)

How to Be Cool in the Third Grade (1993)

How to Be Happy Even When Life Has Other Plans for You (2001)

How to Be Lost (2004)

How to Become a Virgin (1982)

How to Become Extinct (1941)

How to Become King (1977)

How to Become Normal When You're Not, and How to Stay Normal When You Are (1999)

How to Become Popular Without Losing Your Mind (2000)

How to Become Super-Spiritual or Kill Yourself Trying (1982)

How to Become Your Own Doctor (1884)

How to Bewitch (2001)

How to Boil Water (1976)

How to Break Out of Prison (2003)

How to Break the Ten Commandments (1977)

How to Bribe a Judge (2002)

How to Bring Up 2000 Teenagers (1979)

How to Build a City (1872)

How to Build a Dinosaur (1997)

How to Build a Flattie or Sharpie (1902)

How to Build Your Own Caravan (1952)

How to Burn (1903)

How to Burn Your Candle (1978)

How to Bury a Millionaire (1999)

How to Bury Your Goods (1999)

How to Buy an Elephant (1977)

How to Catch an Elephant (1999)

How to Cook Everything (1998)

How to Cook Husbands (1899)

How to Create Your Own Painted Lady (1989)

How to Deep-Freeze a Mammoth (1986)

How to Dig a Hole to the Other Side of the World (1979)

How to Disappear Completely and Never Be Found (2002)

How to Do Just About Anything (1986)

How to Dunk a Doughnut (2003)

How to Eat an Elephant (1992)

How to Eat Fried Worms (1973)

How to Embalm Your Mother-in-Law (1993)

How to Fabricate Damn Near Anything (2005)

How to Fail Successfully (1982)

How to Fight a Girl (1987)

How to Get a Gorilla Out of Your Bathtub (2006)

How to Grow Fresh Air (1997)

How to Haunt a House (1994)

How to Hold a Crocodile (1981)

How to Iron Your Own Damn Shirt (2005)

How to Keep a Gorilla (1968)

How to Kill a Monster (1996)

How to Kill Your Girlfriend's Cat (1988)

How to Label a Goat (2006)

How to Lie with Maps (1991)

How to Live Forever (2001)

How to Lose All Your Friends (1994)

How to Lose Your Ass and Regain Your Life (2005)

How to Make an Apple Pie and See the World (1994)

How to Meet Aliens (2001)

How to Murder the Man of Your Dreams (1995)

How to Overthrow the Government (2000)

How to Raise a Brat (1946)

How to Raise a Jewish Dog (2007)

How to Reason Infallibly (1900)

How to Ride a Tiger (1983)

How to Ruin Your Life (2002)

How to Ruin Your Sister's Life (2006)

How to Rule the World (1971)

How to Rule the World for Fun and Profit (2004)

How to Run a Bassoon Factory (1934)

How to Run a War (1972)

How to Seduce a Ghost (2005)

How to Shit in the Woods (1994)

How to Suppress Women's Writing (1983)

How to Talk Back to Your Television Set (1970)

How to Tell a Blackbird from a Sausage (2007)

How to Tell a Naked Man What to Do (2004)

How to Tell if Your Boyfriend is the Antichrist (2007)

How to Tell the Birds from the Flowers (1907)

How to Tell Your Friends from the Apes (1931)

How to Tempt a Fish (1957)

How to Test Your Cat's IQ (1984)

How to Think About Weird Things (2002)

How to Think Like Leonardo Da Vinci (1998)

How to Throw a *!!?+*@!!?+!&*+#!! Golf Club!!! (2008)

How to Torture Your Friends (1941)

How to Torture Your Husband (1948)

How to Torture Your Wife (1948)

How to Travel With a Salmon (1994)

How to Trick or Treat in Outer Space (2004)

How to Understand Propaganda (1952)

How to Wait for Jesus (1979)

How to Walk a Pig (2006)

How to Walk on Water (1992)

How to Walk With Your Hands in Your Pockets (1991)

How to Waste Time Brilliantly (2001)

How to Work Wonders With One Pound of Meat (1979)

How to Worry Successfully (1936)

How to Wreck a Building (1982)

How to Write So That You Cannot Possibly Be Misunderstood (1978)

Daniel Wait Howe (1839-1920)

Gerald Edward Howling (fl. 1937)

Robert T. Howling (fl. 1954)

Ursula Phalla Hubbard (b. 1904)

Lina Hug (fl. 1890)

Otto Hugger (fl. 1960) [He loved cars.]

Viktor Hugger (fl. 1918) [He loved winners.]

William Hung (b. 1893)

Herbert Hunger (b. 1914)

John Hunkey (d. 1917)

Melissa Dearing Jack Hurt (b. 1911)

Marc Gabriel Hurt-Binet (fl. 1862)

Hugo Hurter (1832-1914)

Bill Hurtz (b. 1919)

Dick Hyman (b. 1907)

I

Ibn Shit al-Qurashi (fl. 12th century)

William Ick (fl. 1842)

S.S. Ick-Hewins (fl. 1938)

Eugene Clutterbuck Impey (fl. 1865)

Howard von Hardenberg Inches (b. 1910)

INDENTURED SERVANTS [Those are the
ones with false teeth.]

Bärbel Inhelder (fl. 1958)

Queenie Iredale (fl. 1935)

The Island of Menstruating Men (1970)

Orange Jacobs (1827-1914)

Philibert Jambe de Fer (d. 1572)

Beat R. Jenny (fl. 1959)

Ingeborg Jerk (fl. 1923)

Wiking Jerk (fl. 1947)

John Leech on My Shelves (1930)

Skull Johnson (fl. 1948)

John Beer Johnstone (1803-1891) [Beer is his middle name!]

Douglas Waddell Jolly (fl. 1940)

Julius Jolly (1849-1932)

Lloyd Peniston Jones (b. 1884)

Cock de Jong (fl. 1951)

Misse Worm Jørgensen (fl. 1943)

Erin Elver Jucker-Fleetwood (fl. 1958)

Orange Judd (1822-1892)

Beat Junker (fl. 1955)

Jurnal of Helth: A Monthly Magazine Devoted to the Promotion of Helth [sic] (1891-1892)

Sol Felty Light (1886-1947)

Charles Earl Limp (fl. 1920)

Lorenzo Lippi (1606-1664)

Theodor Lipps (1851-1914)

Grace Elizabeth Lippy (b. 1901)

The Origin of Things (1947) by Julius Lips
    (1895-1950) and Eva Lips (b. 1906)

Elena Emmanuilovna Lipshits (fl. 1951)

Frédéric Gustave Lix (fl. 1869)

Emma Lard Longan (b. 1854)

Henry Wadsworth Longfellow (1807-1882)

Stephen Hemsley Longrigg (fl. 1953)

Floyd Looney (b. 1906)

J. Thomas Looney (fl. 1921)

Morgan Harbin Looney (1825-1901)

Myrtle Owens Looney (fl. 1936)

Zolon Marion Looney (b. 1916)

Cornelis Loots (1765-1834)

Guillermo López Hipkiss (fl. 1935)

Abram Mironovich Lopshits (fl. 1956)

John E. Loser (fl. 1940)

Grover Cleveland Loud (1890-1968)

John Adams Loud (fl. 1898)

Marguerite St. Leon Barstow Loud (1812?-
    1889)

LOUD FAMILY

Herry Lovelich (fl. 1450)

Samuel Lover (1797-1868)

Bertram V.A. Low-Beer (fl. 1950)

Oswald Swinney Lowsley (b. 1884)

Peter Lung (1768-1816)

Wilhelm Lürken (fl. 1911)

Manfred Lurker (fl. 1958)

Sir Montague Lush (1853-1930)

*The Concealed Sins: Wastes of Health of
    Suffering Humanity: Sexual Diseases,
    Their Prevention and Cure from a
    Medical and Biblical Standpoint*
    (1926) by El Lernanto, with supple-
    ment on sexual diseases and birth
    control by Benedict Lust (b. 1872)

Return to Nature! (1903) by Adolf Just,
    translated by Benedict Lust (b. 1872)

Edgar Lustgarten (1907-1978)

Lying for Fun and Profit (1999)

Mary Tyler Freeman Cheek McClenahan (b.
    1917)

Silas Bent McKinley (b. 1893)

Perley McNutt (fl. 1972)

Pedro de Madrazzo y Kuntz (1816-1898)

Nila Ivanovna Shevko Magidoff (b. 1905)

Gholamreza Mahboubi (fl. 1970)

Making Medicine (1844-1931)

Boo von Malmborg (fl. 1956)

The Building of a Nation (1911) by May Rid-
    path Mann and Mary Engstrom Hoss
    [Men and hosses workin' together.]

Criticism of Marx's Economic Theory (1927)
    by Mao Yi Poo

Claude Marks (fl. 1957)

Ernest Marriage (fl. 1901)

Semen Iosifovich Mashinskii (fl. 1952)

Cotton Mather (1663-1728)

Increase Mather (1639-1723)

Archie Birdsong Mathews (fl. 1952)

Charles Geekie Matthew (fl. 1911)

Matthew Holmes Mawhinney (b. 1889)

Rev. Experience Mayhew (1673-1758)

Ralph Eugene Meatyard (1925-1972)

Arthur Mee (1875-1943)

Carroll Louis Vanderslice Meeks (1907-1966)

V.B. Meen (fl. 1959) [Vell, ve be nice!]

DeForest Mellon (fl. 1934)

Prosper Mérimée (1803-1870)

A Method for Distinguishing the Sex of Young Chicks (1923)

Ross Raymond Middlemiss (fl. 1946)

Marten Micron (1523-1559)

The Minor Structures of Deformed Rocks (1972)

César de Missy (1703-1775)

Nat de Mons (fl. 13th century)

Charles Anthony Moo (fl. 1959)

Booth Mooney (b. 1912)

Agatho Moons (1888-1953)

Banner Bill Morgan (1915-1950)

Bernice Bangs Morgan (fl. 1952)

Harry Titterton Morgan (b. 1872)

Rising Lake Morrow (b. 1901)

Edward Ratcliffe Garth Russell Evans, Baron Mountevans (1880-1957)

Peter Muck (b. 1870)

Richard Muck (fl. 1943)

Henry Muddiman (1628-29? - 1692)

Christian Fürchtegott Muff (1841-1911)

Lodowick Muggleton (1609-1698)

Jean Bernard Muschi (b. 1847)

Patrizio Muschi (fl. 1826)

Harry Stoll Mustard (1889-1966)

Wilfred Pirt Mustard (1864-1932)

Maurice Mutterer (fl. 1930)

Eadweard Muybridge (1830-1904)

Denis Mycock (fl. 1960)

N

Theres Nasty (fl. 1952)

Bishop Friedrich Nausea (d. 1552)

Salmon of the Pacific Northwest (1958) by
      Anthony Netboy

Solomon Netboy (fl. 1928)

Clam Neuburg (fl. 1876) [Did he have a
      brother named Lobster?]

*New and Gorgeous Pantomime Entitled
      Harlequin Prince Cherry Top and the
      Good Fairy Fairfuck: or, The Frig, the
      Fuck, and the Fairy* (1879) by George
      Augustus Henry Fairfield Sala

A New Catalogue of Vulgar Errors (1767)

Idus A. Newby (fl. 1957)

World Government (1942) by Oscar
      Newfang (b. 1875)

Clarence Bobo Nickels (b. 1898)

The No Asshole Rule (2007)

C.B. Noisy (fl. 1857)

Asaji Nose (1894-1955)
Karl Wilhelm Nose (1753?-1835)
Zebedee Nungak (fl. 1969)
Henry Lightfoot Nunn (b. 1878)

Shatswell Ober (1894-1985)
Anna Frances Odor (b. 1920)
Buford Odor (fl. 1957)
Frank Odor (fl. 1954)
Paul Odor (fl. 1942)
Ralph K. Odor (fl. 1935)
Susan Frances Tyler Odor (b. 1842)
J.P. O'Fake (fl. 1910)
Elizabeth Off (fl. 1957)
Marbury Bladen Ogle (b. 1910)
Fred Lowell Ogles (fl. 1935)
Gilbert Donald Ogles (fl. 1952)
J.M. Old (fl. 1945)
William Abbott Oldfather (1880-1945)
Smith Hempstone Oliver (fl. 1956)
Pierre Robert Olivetan (1500-1538)

Brian O'Looney (fl. 1876)

Orange A. Olsen (1890-1945)

Oliver Onions (1873-1961)

Simon O'Queer (fl. 1757)

Florence E. Orange (fl. 1929)

Ants Oras (b. 1900)

Robert Henri and his Circle (1969) by
William Innes Homer with the
assistance of Violet Organ

Giacomo Orifice (1865-1922)

Susan Wealthy Orvis (1873-1941)

Augustine John Osgniach (b. 1891)

Hildegard Budnick Ostapowicz (fl. 1951)

Marguerite Claverie Ekdahl Oswald (b. 1907)

César Antonovich Oui (1835-1918)

Jules Oui (fl. 1894)

Outfox the Kids for Fun and Profit (2007)

Albert Timothy Outlaw (b. 1894)

Algee Currie Outlaw (fl. 1950)

Beville S. Outlaw, Jr. (b. 1924)

David Outlaw (1806-1868)

Donald Elmer Outlaw (b. 1919)

Doris Croom Outlaw (b. 1915)

Mary Van Outlaw (fl. 1960)

Julia P. Outhouse (fl. 1932)

Antoinette Arnolda Overman (fl. 1933)

John Cockey Owings (fl. 1790)

Kunt Ozan (fl. 1937)

Grassblade Jungle (1959) by Nesta Pain (b. 1905)

Some Methods of Marketing Milk in Ohio (1930) by Aaron J. Pancake

Manual of Sugar Data (1932) by J.D. Pancake

Loral Wilford Pancake (fl. 1951)

Mary Susan Parsons Pancake (1847-1923)

Mollie Panter-Downes (1906-1997)

Carl Frederick Abel Pantin (1899-1967)

William Abel Pantin (b. 1902)

J. Harwood Panting (fl. 1889)

Peter James Panting (fl. 1953)

John Papajohn (fl. 1956)

Viola Paradise (b. 1887) [Accordion hell?]

Sir Woodbine Parish (1796-1882)

André Parrot (b. 1901)

Peter Partner (fl. 1958)

Richard A. Passwater (fl. 1967)

Coventry Kersey Dighton Patmore (1823-1896)

Sidney Patzer (fl. 1932)

Thomas Love Peacock (1785-1866)

Jean Claude Pecker (fl. 1954)

P. Pecker (fl. 1904)

Sophie Pecker (fl. 1915)

Charlotte Pecker-Wimel (fl. 1953)

Else Pée (fl. 1933)

Ernst Pée-Laby (fl. 1915)

P. van Pée (fl. 1947)

Hedley Peek (fl. 1897)

Daniel Peenius (1622-1680)

Max Minor Peet (fl. 1909)

Robert Barfe Peet (fl. 1925)

Ida Maharadjadewata Anak Agung Gede Pemeregan (fl. 1960)

John Devitt Stringfellow Pendlebury (1904-1941)

Fernand Pénissou (fl. 1883)

Edwin Harness Penisten (fl. 1958)

Hattie Walters Penisten (fl. 1933)

The Kinetics of Rubber Vulcanization (1933) by Quinton Pearman Peniston

Reinzi Evylin Peniston (b. 1850)

Roger Peniston-Bird (fl. 1959)

Areal Extent and Thickness of the Salt Deposits of Ohio (1947) by James F. Pepper

Mary Sifton Pepper (d. 1908)

Hazel Perfect (fl. 1959)

Mariano Perfecto (b. 1858)

Doyt L. Perry (fl. 1938)

Stow Persons (b. 1913)

Bruno Perversi (fl. 1839)

Volkert Pfaff (fl. 1927)

Melchior Pfintzing (1481-1535)

Eden Phillpotts (1862-1960)

PHONY PEACH DISEASE

Philip Syng Physick (1768-1837)

Dorothy Maud Pickles (fl. 1960)

Marie Luise Cuntz Picot (b. 1910)

Pictures of Travel in the South of France, Illustrated (1950) [Well, duh!]

Oliver Pigg (b. ca. 1551)

Thomas Strangeways Pigg-Strangeways (1866-1926)

Augustus Penn Pigman (fl. 1938)

Walter Griffith Pigman (1818-1892)

Chemistry of the Carbohydrates (1948) by William Ward Pigman (b. 1910)

Max Pimpl (fl. 1938)

Jenny O'Hara Pincock (fl. 1930)

Lowell Dalling Pincock (fl. 1954)

Henry de Worms, Baron Pirbright (1840-1903)

The Piss-Pot: A Copy of Verses on a Silver Chamber-Pot Sent to the Tower to be Coyned, Occasion'd by the Lady _____ at St. James's Unlucky Hand at Basset, Which Forc'd Her to Sell Her Plate (1701)

The Pisse-Prophet, or, Certain Pisse-Pot Lectures: Wherein Are Newly Discovered the Old Fallacies, Deceit, and Jugling of the Piss-Pot Science, Used by All Those (Whether Quacks, and Empiricks, or Other Methodical Physicians) Who Pretend Knowledge of Diseases, by the Urine, in Giving Judgement of the Same (1679)

Marcel Pisseau (fl. 1927)

Ludwig Pissel (b. 1885)

Vegetio A. Pisseni (fl. 1641)

Désiré Pissens (1881-1955)

Robert Pissère (fl. 1943)

Eugen Raym Pissin (fl. 1874)

Raimund Pissin (b. 1878)

Georges Pisson (fl. 1892)

Noël Laurent Pissot (1770?-1815)

Pauline-Marguerite Pissot-Masson (fl. 1920)

Robert Pissoy (fl. 1781)

Panduronga S. S. Pissurlencar (fl. 1933)

Augustus Henry Lane-Fox Pitt-Rivers
     (1827-1900)

George Henry Lane-Fox Pitt-Rivers (b.
     1890)

Rosalind Venetia Pitt-Rivers (fl. 1960)

Thad Heckle Pittenger (fl. 1951)

James Robert Soda Pitts (b. 1833)

Lilla Belle Pitts (fl. 1950)

William Savage Pitts (1830-1918)

Isabel Pizza de Luna (fl. 1958)

Vito Pizza (fl. 1597)

Perley Oakland Place (1872-1946)

Plaster Casting for Fun and Profit (1966)
     [Did this inspire Cynthia Albritton?]

Lyon Playfair, Baron Playfair (1818-1898)

Sir Robert Lambert Playfair (1828-1899)

Daisy, Fürstin von Pless (1873-1943)

Raoul Plus (1882-1958)

Peter Pomp (fl. 1868)

Gerald Mungo Ponton (b. 1888)

José Alfredo Póo Zepeda (fl. 1951)

José de Poo (1831-1898)

Ping Nan Poo (fl. 1895)

Thomas Poo (fl. 1780)

Alfons Poope (fl. 1918)

J. Poopuu (fl. 1921)

Stale Popov (1902-1965)

Percivall Pott (1714-1788)

John Potts (1838-1907)

Hortense Powdermaker (1903-1970)

Albany Poyntz (fl. 1845)

Launce Poyntz (fl. 1875)

Newdigate Poyntz (fl. 1872)

George Leonard Prestige (b. 1889)

Franciscus Petrus Hubertus Prick van
      Wely (1867-1926)

Max Arthur Prick van Wely (b. 1909)

Hellmuth Pricks (fl. 1931)

Thomas Carew Esquire, One of the
      Gentlemen of the Privie-Chamber,
      and Sewer in Ordinary to His
      Majesty (1595?-1639?)

Thomas Fullalove Probey (b. 1895)

Songling Pu (1640-1715)

Bertram S. Puckle (fl. 1926)

Ralph Pudd (b. 1879)

Alexander Puff (b. 1887)

A.M. Puke (fl. 1928) [Like clockwork, every
      morning.]

J. Puke (fl. 1802)

Sven Puke (fl. 1916)

Peter Rose Pulham (1910-1956)

PULSATING STARS — CONGRESSES

Ernst Punks (fl. 1938)

Snell Wallace Putney (fl. 1951)

Louis Joseph Putz (b. 1909)

Walter Lytle Pyle (1871-1921)

Hendrik Peter Godfried Quack (1834-1917)

A. Quapp (fl. 1864)

Edgar Monsanto Queeny (1897-1968)

Cruising Southeastern Alaska (1945) by Ethel S. Queeny

Archibald Queer (fl. 1916)

Elmer Roy Queer (fl. 1930)

Herbert Quick (1861-1925)

Oliver Chase Quick (1885-1944)

Hugh Richard Heathcote Gascoyne-Cecil, Baron Quickswood (1869-1956)

Sir Arthur Thomas Quiller-Couch (1863-1944)

Georg Hermann Quincke (1834-1924)

Randolph Quirk (fl. 1957)

William Quirk (1881-1926)

Raise Crickets for Fun and Profit (1949)

Raising Children for Fun and Profit (1987)

John Ramsbottom (b. 1885)

Richard Rank (fl. 1949)

Maurice Rat (fl. 1957)

Richard Updegraff Ratcliff (b. 1906)

Denise Ravage (fl. 1950)

Marcus Eli Ravage (1884-1965)

Gough Raw (fl. 1966)

Henri Roux de Raze (1790-1863)

John Rechy (fl. 1970)

Juvenile Delinquency (1932), *Vice in Chicago*
(1933), and *Criminal Behavior* (1940)
all by Walter Cade Reckless

Edwin Redslob (1884-1973)

Remains of the Rev. Edmund D. Griffin
(1831) compiled by Francis Griffin
with a biographical memoir of the
deceased by the Rev. John McVickar
[Was Francis Griffin a licensed
mortician?]

Remedying Rip-Offs for Fun and Profit
(1987)

Glad Reusch (fl. 1951)

A Review of the Literature of the Dugong
(1975) [How did they learn to write?]

Rush Rhees (1860-1939)

Rush Rhees (1905-1989)

Pedro Richardson Kuntz (fl. 1931)

Victor von Richter (1841-1891)

James Fred Rippy (b. 1892)

Carl Coke Rister (1889-1955)

Jane Beaglehole Ritchie (fl. 1957)

RIVERS — CONGRESSES [Usually held in
Pittsburgh.]

Johnnie Mae Bugg Roberts (fl. 1953)

Thomas Balling Robertson (1779-1828)

Henry Crabb Robinson (1775-1867)

About Money (1934) by Eric Roll, Baron
Roll of Ipsden (b. 1907)

Duane Henry Du Bose Roller (b. 1920)

*The Romance and Drama of the Rubber
Industry* (1932)

John Wellborn Root (1850-1891)

Vingt-un Rosado (b. 1920)

Peter Rose (fl. 1923)

Strange Ross (fl. 1964)

Marianus Rot (1597-1663)

Lix Rotis (fl. 1892)

Brain Rotman (fl. 1966)

A.H.D. Rots (fl. 1950)

B.D. Rots (fl. 1950)

Ludwig Schnorr von Carolsfeld (b. 1903)

Michael Puff von Schrick (ca. 1400-1473)

Beat Schweingruber (fl. 1955)

Orange Scott (1800-1847)

William Benjamin Screws (b. 1884)

Milvoy S. Seacat (d. 1997)

Ezra Champion Seaman (1805-1880) [The best sailor in the world.]

Valentine Seaman (1770-1817)

Fish Culture for Fun and Profit (1954) by W.R. Seaman

Carl Emil Seashore (1866-1949)

Ferris L. Seashore (fl. 1948)

Rose E. Selfe (b. 1852)

Wanna Sell (fl. 1952)

Señor Bum in the Jungle (1932)

Sewer [pseudonym of Ignacy Maciejowski] (1835-1901)

Sex and the College Student (1969) by Josiah Stinkney Carberry (b. 1929) [Off-center spine title reads *Sex and the College Stud* on some copies.]

Harold Shames (fl. 1948)

Florence Nightingale Horner Sherk (b. 1859)

Hill Shine (b. 1901)

Yusuf Shit (fl. 1886)

Lazar Shitnitzky (b. 1894)

Mosheh Shitrug (d. 1927)

B.P. Shitt (fl. 1938)

Petr Genrikhovich Shitt (1875-1950)

Rev. Robert Shittler (fl. 1853)

Hayim ben Yozpa Shitts (fl. 1863)

James Thomson Shotwell (1874-1965) [Yes, but was he a good dancer?]

Memoirs of the Late Rev. Joseph Horsey (1803) by John Shoveller [*et al.*]

Benjamin Silliman (1779-1864)

Abraham-Justin Silly (b. 1751)

Cephas Hempstone Sinclair (1847-1920)

Suk-Chu Sin (1417-1475)

Satya Brat Sinha (b. 1926)

Johann Rudolf Sinner (1730-1787)

Peter Sinner (fl. 1927)

Vincent Rudolf Meinrad von Sinner (fl. 1955)

Ndabaningi Sithole (b. 1920)

Lamoraal Ulbo de Sitter (b. 1902)

Dame Edith Sitwell (1887-1964)

Hervey Degge Wilmot Sitwell (b. 1896)

Osbert Sitwell (1892-1969)

Sacheverell Sitwell (1897-1988)

Bozo Skerlj (fl. 1950)

John Henry Skinkle (fl. 1949)

Skinny-Dipping for Fun and Profit (1997)

Nils Nilsson Skum (1872-1951)

C.E. Skunk (fl. 1731)

Karl Skunk (fl. 1692)

L.C.L.W. Sloth Blaauboer (fl. 1926)

Edward Slow (1841-1925)

Alexander Smellie (1857-1923)

Kingsley Bryce Speakman Smellie (1897-1987)

William Smellie (1697-1763)

William Smellie (1740-1795)

Marshall Smelser (1955)

Samuel Smiles (1812-1904)

Elephant Smith (fl. 1682)

Preserved Smith (1880-1941)

Jacob Z. Smoker (b. 1890)

Jan Christiaan Smuts (1870-1950)

William Snake (fl. 1859)

Roscoe Raymond Snapp (1889-1953)

Ernst Snapper (b. 1913)

Pseudo-Tuberculosis in Man (1938) by Isidore Snapper (b. 1889) and Arnold Willem Maria Pompen [Pathologists call tuberculosis bacillae "red snappers."]

Mayce Cannon Sneed (b. 1886)

Pitje Snot (fl. 1896)

Abraham Kenneth Snowman (b. 1919)

Edgar Sober (b. 1859)

James Thrall Soby (1906-1979)

Isabella Caroline Somer-Cocks, Lady
        Somerset (1851-1921)

The Korean-Canadian Folk Song (1974) by
        Bang-Song Song

William Swan Sonnenschein (1855-1931)

Soranus (fl. 2nd century) [He was a gyneco-
        logist, but maybe he should have
        tried proctology.]

Kellogg Speed (b. 1879)

Cornelia Mary Speedy (fl. 1884)

Thomas Speedy (1846-1924)

Willy Spillebeen (b. 1932)

Gabriel Spillebout (fl. 1968)

Nicolaas Bartholomeus Petrus Spit (fl. 1889)

Hans Spitzy (b. 1872)

Jerzy Splawa-Neyman (1894-1981)

Rev. Rudolph Alfred Richard Spread (fl.
        1936)

Kenneth Stephen Spreadbury (fl. 1944)

Ernest Spring (fl. 1911)

Sir Cecil Spring Rice (1859-1918)

Anne Louise Germaine Necker, Baroness de Stäel-Holstein (1766-1817)

Karoline Dumpf Stahl (fl. 1817)

Frances Helena Swan Stallybrass (b. 1885)

John Stands in Timber (1882-1967)

Calvin Klopp Staudt (fl. 1909)

Lawrence Dinkelspiel Steefel (b. 1894)

Andreas Erici Stenchelstrup (d. 1678)

Poyntz Stewart (1797-1827)

Regine Kronacher Stix (b. 1895)

Ernest Looney Stockton (b. 1888)

Alvin Theorin Stolen (fl. 1941)

Kermit L. Stolen (fl. 1933)

Victor Otto Stomps (1897-1970)

Joke Stook (1927?-1950)

The Story of Photography (1898) by Alfred Thomas Story (1842-1934)

Edward Fairbrother Strange (1862-1929)

Thomas Bland Strange (1831-1925)

Ralph Beaver Strassburger (1883-1959)

Kathleen Balls Stratton (fl. 1948)

A Stress Analysis of a Strapless Evening Gown (1963)

Thornton Stringfellow (fl. 1861)

Sylvan Irving Stroock (b. 1886)

Hudson Stuck (1863-1920)

Hans Heinz Stuckenschmidt (b. 1901)

Charles Thomas Studd (1860-1931)

Edward Fairfax Studd (fl. 1889)

Grace Hermione Stuff (fl. 1938)

Henry Spencer Stuff (fl. 1926)

Clayton LeRoy Stunkard (fl. 1959)

Horace Wesley Stunkard (b. 1889)

Wilbur Rufus Stunkard (b. 1906)

Charles Inches Sturgis (b. 1860)

Christian Sucker (fl. 1956)

Elfriede Sucker (fl. 1952)

Heinz Sucker (fl. 1955)

Ilse Sucker (fl. 1945)

Immanuel Sucker (fl. 1960)

Joachim Sucker (fl. 1948)

Johann Matthaeus Sucker (fl. 1758)

Karl Friedrich Wilhelm Sucker (fl. 1930)

Ludwig Sucker (fl. 1895)

Sophie Sucker (fl. 1910)

Wilhelm Sucker (fl. 1924)

Wolfgang Sucker (fl. 1953)

Jerome Suckle (fl. 1949)

Margaret Suckley (1891-1991)

Alfred Inigo Suckling (1796-1856)

Sir John Suckling (1609-1642)

A.K. Suckov (fl. 1951)

Lorenz Johann Daniel Suckow (1722-1801)

Ruth Suckow (1892-1960)

Ivan Suk (fl. 1920)

Sushi Sukewaki (1707-1772)

Helena Sukkau (fl. 1920)

Oline Sukkestad (fl. 1955)

Perl Sukonik (fl. 1930)

J.J. van der Sulk (fl. 1799)

Super Worms for Fun and Profit (1973)

Superior Limericks (1976) by Irving
    Superior

Kerry Leyne Supple (fl. 1899)

Nancy Graves Ball Surface (b. 1871)

William Ball Sutch (1907-1975)

Alejandro Sux (1888-1959)

Cleon Oliphant Swayzee (b. 1903)

*The Sweet Potato Queens' Guide to Raising
    Children for Fun and Profit* (2008)

Henry Savage Sweetman (fl. 1875)

Luke Decatur Sweetman (b. 1867)

Paul Marlor Sweezy (1910-2004)

David Swing (1830-1894)

Raymond Swing (1887-1968)

Carl Brent Swisher (1897-1968)

T

Gladys Bagg Taber (b. 1899)

Wilson Hamilton Tackaberry (d. 1910)

Catherine Bridget Tancock (fl. 1959)

Ernest Osborne Tancock (fl. 1919)

Leonard William Tancock (fl. 1949)

Osborne William Tancock (b. 1839)

Hotty Tang (fl. 1949)

Gunnar Tank (b. 1878) [Cf. Gregers Krabbe.]

Increase Niles Tarbox (1815-1888)

Selim Sirri Tarcan (1874-1956?)

Penny Capitalism (1953) by Sol Tax (b. 1907)

Ordway Tead (1891-1973)

Kefton Harding Teague (b. 1920)

Faithful Teate (b. 1621)

Grant Teats (fl. 1939)

Mary E. Teats (fl. 1906)

Roscoe Teats (fl. 1959)

A Technique for the Sex Determination of Chicks (1947)

Anna Teerlink-Muschi (fl. 1819)

Negley King Teeters (b. 1896)

Herbert Mortimer Teets (b. 1872)

Telling Lies for Fun and Profit (1981)

Richard Carnal Temple (fl. 1903)

The Theoretical Child: A Proof of Pre-Natal Influence (1910?) as propounded by Dr. J.W. Coffey (skeleton dude of U.S.A. and the Old World); also the story of his life, travels, and marriage, and sketch of his daughter, Elsie Coffee by Dr. D.T. Elliott [sic]

Leprosy (1891) by George Thin

Robert Thin (fl. 1927)

Curtis Willard Thing (b. 1894)

Eric Thing (fl. 1955)

John Thing (fl. 1810)

Samuel Thing (d. 1831?)

Lately Thomas (1898-1977)

John Ebenezer Honeyman Thomson (1841-1923)

Thomas Bangs Thorpe (1815-1878)

Albert Thumb (1865-1915)

Moses ibn Tibbon (fl. 13th century)

Sister Alphonse Marie Tickler (fl. 1946)

Charles Meymott Tidy (1843-1892)

A Little about Leech (1931) by Gordon Tidy

Sir Henry Letheby Tidy (b. 1877)

Hilda Tiger (fl. 1960)

Edward John Tilt (1815-1893)

Tin-Tummi: or, The Prehistoric War (1917)

Thomas Tissue (fl. 1969)

Anton Emil Titl (1809-1882)

Initiation à la biologie (1928) and *Notre vie physique* (1933), both by Désiré Tits

Généralisations des groupes projectifs (1949) and *Buildings of Spherical Type and Finite BN-Pairs* (1974), both by Jacques Tits

Dorothy Elizabeth Titt (fl. 1932)

Edwin Warren Titt (b. 1907)

LeVata Titt (fl. 1939)

Herbert Titter (fl. 1946)

Anne Montague Titterington (fl. 1927)

Julius Tittmann (1814-1883)

George Francis Titterton (b. 1904)

Joy Tivy (fl. 1958)

Yuk Sam Tom (fl. 1921)

Pin Tong (fl. 1924)

Hollington Kong Tong (1887-1971)

Thomas H. Tongue (1844-1903)

Granville Toogood (b. 1899)

Selwyn Toogood (b. 1916)

Arthur Tooth (1914-1942)

Charles Robinson Toothaker (1873-1952)

Harry King Tootle (fl. 1947)

Rev. Augustus Montague Toplady (1740-1778)

Tomato Cookery (1951) by Eva Topping
(1898-1951) [Whatever she put on
those tomatoes must have killed her.]

Salem Town (1779-1864)

Rev. Robert Trail, Rector of Skull (fl. 1837)

*Trapping Alfalfa Leafcutter Bees for Fun
and Profit* (1969)

Kerith Lloyd Kinsey Trick (fl. 1968)

Connally Findlay Trigg (1810-1880)

Gratianus Trimmer (fl. 1689)

John Dezendorf Trimmer (b. 1907) [Have
you had your dezendorf trimmed
recently?]

Felix von Trojan (1895-1968)

Like a Watered Garden (1954) by Jessie
Mary Trout (1895-1990)

Webster Prentiss True (b. 1892)

*Deformities, Including Diseases of the
Bones and Joints: A Text-Book of
Orthopaedic Surgery* (1912) by Alfred
Herbert Tubby (b. 1862)

Daniel Hack Tuke (1827-1895)

The Insanity of Over-Exertion of the Brain
(1894) by Sir John Batty Tuke
(1835-1913)

Alfred William Peniston Tulip (fl. 1952)

Ottokar Anton Alois Tumlirz (b. 1856)

Thin Tun (fl. 1960)

Orhan Tuna (b. 1909)

Turdy (d. 1699)

Midge Turk (fl. 1971)

Milton Haight Turk (1866-1949)

Willie Anne Cary Turk (fl. 1909)

Ahmad Riyad Turki (fl. 1959)

Bakbars Turki (d. 1254)

Turk 'Ali Shah Qalandar Turki Nur-Mahalli (fl. 1912)

Husayn Turki Shirazi (fl. 1893)

Brinton Turkle (fl. 1958)

Parmenas Taylor Turnley (1821-1911)

Ethel Brilliana Harley Tweedie (d. 1940)

Titus Twitcher (fl. 1792)

Poyntz Tyler (fl. 1956)

Sewell Tappan Tyng (1895-1946)

Walter Ueberwasser (b. 1898)

Cave Underhill (1634-1710?)

Albrecht Unsöld (b. 1905)

Anne Liddell FitzRoy FitzPatrick, Countess of Upper Ossory (1737-38? - 1804)

Edward Upward (b. 1903)

Michelangelo Vaginari, Bishop of Giovenazzo (d. 1667)

Konstantin Vaginov (1899-1934)

Annie Ellen Vanderslice (fl. 1930)

Ely Van de Warker (1841-1910)

Dale Van Every (b. 1896)

Edward Bunn Van Ormer (b. 1903)

Amos Van Wart (fl. 1864)

Evelyn Van Wart (fl. 1898)

Geraldine Van Wart (fl. 1922)

Horace Hume Van Wart (fl. 1931)

Irving Van Wart, Jr. (fl. 1864)

Lizzie D. Van Wart (fl. 1900)

Reginald Bramley Van Wart (fl. 1926)

Petrus Vanderanus (fl. 1560)

Queenie Verity-Steele (fl. 1949)

Coolie Verner (fl. 1960)

Bozo Vidoeski (fl. 1953)

Ants Viires (fl. 1960)

Maxine Boord Virtue (fl. 1956)

Nico G. Vlot (fl. 1952)

G. Vlug (fl. 1929)

Work and Motivation (1964) by Victor H. Vroom

Henry Wellington Wack (1869-1954)

Wilhelm Heinrich Wackenroder (1773-1798)

Wolfgang Wacker (fl. 1959)

Hans Beat Wackernael (fl. 1958)

William Wadd (1776-1829)

Angus L. Waddle (b. 1826?)

Charleszetta Waddles (b. 1912)

Horst Wagon (fl. 1939)

Maurice Wagon (fl. 1937)

Miles Walker (1867-1941)

Beatrice Wallop, Countess of Portsmouth
(fl. 1915)

Bernard Wallop (1794-1859)

Douglass Wallop (b. 1920)

Gerard Vernon Wallop, Earl of Portsmouth
(b. 1898)

Gerard Vernon Wallop, Viscount
Lymington (fl. 1938)

Sir Henry Wallop (fl. 1583)

John Charles Wallop, Third Earl of
Portsmouth (fl. 1823)

Ernest Wallwork (fl. 1972)

Will Walter (b. 1866) [Will Walter what?]

Beat Ludwig Walthard (fl. 1782)

Ferdinand Geminian Wanker (1758-1824)

David Warrior (fl. 1911)

A.D.F. van der Wart (fl. 1946)

Dirk Anthony van de Wart (1767-1824)

Georges Wart (fl. 1948)

Jakob von Wart (d. 1331)

W.F.H. van der Wart (fl. 1921)

Harm Tjalling Waterbolk (fl. 1954)

Walter Crum Watson (fl. 1908)

Harry Wax (fl. 1941)

Leslie Dixon Weatherhead (b. 1893)

Batty Weber (1860-1940)

Richard Dick Weber (fl. 1951)

The Wet Sheet (1843) by Samuel Weeding

Rush Welter (fl. 1959)

Eudora Welty (1909-2001)

Fritz Warmolt Went (b. 1903) [Where did he go?]

Wet Phawaphutanon Na Mahasarakham (fl. 1949)

Wet Wutthiphum (fl. 1952)

Paul Wets (fl. 1928)

Penistone Whalley (fl. 1661)

Benjamin Wham (fl. 1917)

Quincy Farr Wham (fl. 1939)

Sukoo Jack Whang (fl. 1960)

Joshua Whatmough (1897-1964)

Pascal Kidder Whelpton (b. 1893)

Guy Montrose Whipple (1876-1941)

Henry Alcock White (1864-1898)

Jon Ewbank Manchip White (b. 1924)

Robert Looney Caruthers White (b. 1844)

Edward Orange Wildman Whitehouse (fl. 1858)

The Island: or, An Adventure of a Person of Quality (1888) by Richard Whiteing (1840-1928)

A Century of Fiction by American Negroes, 1853-1952: A Descriptive Bibliography (1955) and *Gentlemen in Crisis* (1975), both by Maxwell Whiteman

Why I Want to Fuck Ronald Reagan (1968)

Cocky Wiersinga (fl. 1940)

Isabella Councilman Wigglesworth (b. 1895)

Sir Vincent Brian Wigglesworth (b. 1899)

Rosa Wiggli (1901-1991)

Early Days of Coastal Georgia (1955) by Orrin Sage Wightman (b. 1873)

WILD MEN IN LITERATURE [Such as Oscar Wilde?]

Oscar Fingall O'Flahertie Wills Wilde (1854-1900)

Arthur Wesley Wildman (b. 1901)

John Hazard Wildman (1911-1992)

Rounsevelle Wildman (1864-1901)

Willie Wildman (fl. 1853)

Paul Fears Wiley (b. 1916) [Wiley is afraid of Paul too.]

Franc Bangs Wilkie (1832-1892)

Hesper Odor Williams (fl. 1929)

Druid Wilson (b. 1906)

Charlotte Burch Wimp (fl. 1937)

Inversion of Power Series (1959) by Larry L. Wimp

Ruth Wimp (fl. 1924)

Natural History of Birds: A Guide to Ornithology (1956) by Leonard William Wing (b. 1906)

Henry Winkles (1800- ca. 1860)

Joseph Foulkes Winks (1792-1866)

Alban Dewes Winspear (b. 1899)

Wait Still Winthrop (1643-1717)

Philosophy and its Place in Our Culture (1975) by John Oulton Wisdom (b. 1904)

Brownie Wise (fl. 1957)

Jack Welmer Wise (b. 1917)

Minerva Fries Wise (b. 1861)

Harvey Wish (b. 1909)

Bernard W. Wishy (b. 1925)

N. Wiskie (fl. 1963)

Claud Francis Witty (b. 1877)

Paul A. Woke (fl. 1941)

The Philosophy of Nietzsche (1915) by A. Wolf (1876-1948)

Chick Sing Wong (fl. 1872) [Let's teach her to sing wight.]

Anne Swann Woodcock (b. 1860)

Kathleen Louise Wood-Legh (fl. 1956)

John Wooden Legs (fl. 1976)

Fritz Worm (b. 1884)

Fried Hardy Worm (fl. 1920)

Hardy Worm (1896-1973)

Ole Worm (1588-1654)

Piet Worm (1909-1996)

Zeno Hermannus Worm (fl. 1712)

German Worm Lavergne (fl. 1930)

Titia Worm-Wiegman (b. 1913)

Grover Salman Wormer (fl. 1897)

The Earth and its Mechanism (1862) by Henry Worms

Bernard Lister Worsnop (b. 1892)

Henry Slack Worthington (b. 1856)

Skeptical Sociology (1976) by Dennis Hume Wrong (b. 1923)

Edward Murray Wrong (1889-1928)

George McKinnon Wrong (1860-1948)

Bonita Teter Witty (b. 1904)

Margaret Wrong (fl. 1942)

Lillie Buffum Chace Wyman (1847-1929)

Rodrigo Domingo Xinic Bop (fl. 1998)

Meow-Foo Yap (fl. 1958)

Speech of Mr. Yell of Arkansas, on the Bill to Raise Two New Regiments of Riflemen (1846) by Archibald Yell (1797 or 1799 - 1847)

Michel Yell (fl. 1912)

Dan Yelling (fl. 1953)

Georgia Butt Young (1834-1911)

Stark Young (1881-1963)

Sir Francis Edward Younghusband (1863-1942)

Ichigu Yoyo (fl. 1845)

Michel Yoyo (fl. 1958)

Karel Vladislav Zap (1812-1871)

Charles Franklyn Zeek (b. 1886)

Carl Zigrosser (b. 1891)

Karl Zipp (b. 1890)

Albert Zipper (b. 1855)

Bernhard Zipper (fl. 1909)

Eva Maria Zipper (b. 1925)

Ferry Zipper (fl. 1946)

Paul Zipperer (d. 1903)

Charles Carl Zippermann (fl. 1935)

Claude Ephraim ZoBell (b. 1904)

J.P. Zoomers-Vermeer (1880-1968)

ZOONOSES

Joan Zorro (fl. 1250)

Dolfo Zorzut (1894-1960)

Guido Zschokke (fl. 1897)

Maxine Melba Zugg (fl. 1935)

Albert Zugsmith (fl. 1958)

Leane Zugsmith (1903-1969)

Leo Ritter von Zumbusch (b. 1874)

Beat Fidel Zurlauben (1720-1799)

Leopold Frederick Zwarg (b. 1886)

Charles van der Zweep (fl. 1883)

Pius Zwÿssig (1861-1926)

It is my fervent hope that everyone who has a funny name will write a book!